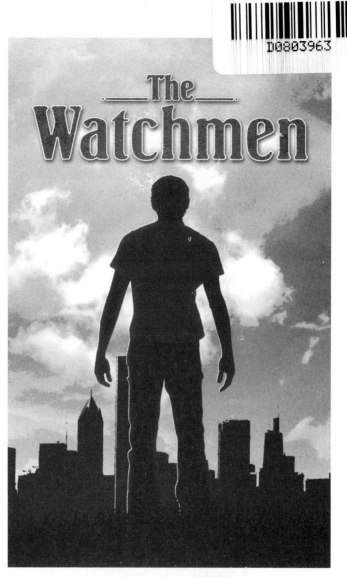

The Watchmen

Mark Cahill

Author of the bestsellers,
One Thing You Can't Do in Heaven
and
One Heartbeat Away

The Watchmen
Mark Cahill

August 2012

ISBN 978-0-578-11076-9

Published by:
    BDM Publishing
    2212 Chisholm Trail
    Rockwall, Texas 75002
    972-771-0568

Bible verses cited are from the King James Version.

Editor:
    Emily L. Foley
    www.EmilyLFoley.com

Cover Design, Interior Illustrations, Page Layout:
    Russell Barr, BARRgraphics
    www.barrgraphics.com

Order additional copies at any bookstore
or at www.markcahill.org.

Printed in the United States of America

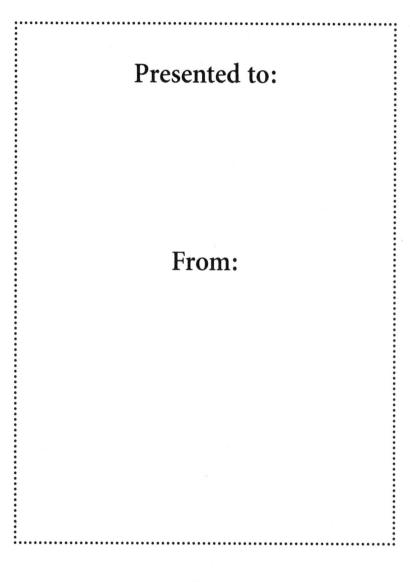

Presented to:

From:

Dedication

*This book is dedicated to the watchmen
who have come before us, the watchmen who
are, and the watchmen who are to come.*

"A watchman cannot remain silent while the world perishes. This book will propel you to reach out to the lost with a sense of urgency as the days run short. *The Watchmen* is a sobering reminder that our brief time on earth is not a time for play, but a battle for the souls of men and women. In these pages, Mark Cahill deeply challenges soldiers of Christ to get out of the sandbox of comfort and march onto the battlefield of this world as faithful watchmen for our Lord Jesus Christ." *–Josh Page, A Watchman*

"This book brings into sharp focus what is closest to God's heart: that His watchmen live sold-out for Him and warn the lost to take refuge in Christ. Take hold of Mark Cahill's outstretched hand as his real-life witnessing stories, punctuated by profound truth, pull your heart up on the wall of God to be a resolute and unashamed watchman calling the perishing to choose life. Incredible encounters and "off the charts" joy await those who do!" *–Brenda Nickel, A Watchman*

"Satan doesn't like Christians, but he hates Mark Cahill's guts. Satan can't fight an army, and this book is a trumpet call to the army of the Lord, to all who call on the name of Jesus Christ…Awaken!" *–Jon Lamb, A Watchman*

"Personal illustrations are the pump-up music I need to keep my Gospel trumpet warmed and tuned. Mark's challenge from Scripture in his newest book, complemented by real personal illustrations of how those Scriptures work in the real world with real people, is for me, everything I need to keep blowing the trumpet of truth with passion. Mark Cahill is a mentor to watchmen." *–Don Blythe, A Watchman*

"This book was not written from the back room based on evangelism theory. Mark has written the most practical, challenge-filled book I've ever read written by man on this subject. Anyone with the Spirit indwelling them can tell this was written by a man with constant witnessing experience and a fear of the Lord.'" *–John Bensley, A Watchman*

"If you want what matters most to God to matter most to you, I believe the message in this book will resonate with you. Tears flood my eyes, as there are no words that can adequately express my gratitude for the faithful watchmen in my life!!!" *–Linda Ruttle, A Watchman*

"*The Watchmen* is so captivating that you won't put it down; so compelling that it will cause you to examine your priorities, and so convicting that it will change the way you live your everyday life. A trumpet blast of truth for the Church of Jesus Christ to wake up–a must read!" *–Dave Farmer, A Watchman*

CONTENTS

Introduction

"When you fear God, you fear nothing else!"[1]
—Oswald Chambers

By the time you finish reading this book, I hope you are very uncomfortable. I wouldn't even have a problem if you didn't like me by the time you set this book down.

You probably didn't expect to read the above two sentences in an introduction for a book. But I wanted to warn you up front: There is a serious challenge coming in the following pages. This book is not for the lighthearted. This book is not for people who want an average existence. If you want to be lukewarm as you follow Jesus Christ, that is your choice. A very bad choice, but your choice nonetheless. We will have decisions to make in this lifetime. Decisions always have consequences: both good and bad.

The pages ahead are for those who want to live a sold out life for the Lord. They are for those who want to make a difference. They are for those that know they don't belong in this world, but are just passing through. They are for those who are *in* the world but not *of* the world. They are for those that have no desire to be mediocre.

My favorite teachers back in school were the ones who wanted me to be a great student and have a hunger for learning. My favorite coaches when I played basketball were the ones who wanted me to be great on a basketball court and didn't want me to be second best. My favorite managers when I was out in the business world were the ones who wanted me to run a great department and be very successful.

The truth of the matter is that my favorite pastors, preachers, and speakers are the ones that want me to be a great man of God who obeys the Lord! It is the people who are willing to step on my toes and aren't overly concerned about my feelings

An unexceptional, standard, run-of-the-mill life for someone who follows Jesus Christ is not acceptable to Him and should not be acceptable to who you see in the mirror each day.

that really motivate me to do my best. My favorite sermons are the ones that as I'm listening, my toes are being crushed, because that man does not want me living an ordinary, middle-of-the-road life. The so-so Christian life is not acceptable to that type of speaker. They cannot be overly concerned about the audience's reaction. They cannot be overly concerned if some people in a congregation say they will turn off the spigot and stop tithing and donating money to the church if they don't tone it down some. Nope, that man of God knows Who he answers to, and it is not anyone that is wrapped in flesh. I thank God for people like that. They have helped make me the man I am today.

I hope the truths and the challenges in this book will do the same thing to you. An unexceptional, standard, run-of-the-mill life for someone who follows Jesus Christ is not acceptable to Him and should not be acceptable to who you see in the mirror each day.

> **Jude 3:** "Beloved, when I gave all diligence to write unto you of the common salvation, it was needful for me to write unto you, and exhort *you* that ye should earnestly contend for the faith which was once delivered unto the saints."

Passionate followers of the Most High God always contend for the faith. If you have never shared your faith before, this book is for you. If you do share your faith a little bit, this book is for you. If you get timid or nervous when talking to a lost person, this book is for you. If you witness everyday of your life, this book is for you.

All I want you to do is to read this book, and then from that moment on, be bolder for reaching the lost for Christ than you ever were before.

Will you join The Watchmen before you take your last breath? You want to be a part of that group. You will find out what a watchman is, and be encouraged to join them before you finish this book. I do hope you enjoy and are challenged by this book. The other Watchmen await to see if you will join the club. But more importantly, the Lord awaits to see if you are going to sign up before you die.

You have
been entrusted with
the eternal truths that everyone
needs to know.

What
are you
doing with
the gospel God
has entrusted
to you?

Chapter 1
Bloodcurdling Scream

"Give me one hundred preachers who fear nothing but sin, and desire nothing but God, and I care not a straw whether they be clergymen or laymen; such alone will shake the gates of hell and set up the kingdom of heaven on Earth."[2]
–John Wesley

Ezekiel 33:1: "Again the word of the LORD came unto me, saying:"

Remember that the Word of the Lord comes to us by God's Word, the Holy Bible. It is the measure you should use to determine if what you are hearing in today's world is truth or not.

The Bible promises that in the end of the days, there will be false christs, false prophets, and false teachers. These are all false religious people. Religious people can be the most dangerous people that you will ever meet. Why? Because most of us do not expect a religious person to deceive us. We assume they will tell us the truth. We let our guards down. Often, we accept anything a religious person says, instead of testing their words against God's Word.

I have heard so many horror stories of students who go off to college and get deceived by their professors. But the worst of those stories is when that deception takes places at Christian colleges. Some students have said that they were taught evolution as fact. Some were taught that the miracles in Exodus never really happened. Well if those didn't happen, why would we believe in the miracle of the forgiveness of sins, or the miracle of the resurrection? You see, those students had their guards down. They trusted their professors more than they trusted the Word of God.

I am telling you right now to keep up your guard as you read this book. Don't trust what I say. Follow what God says. He is the One to whom you will answer. A watchman always has his guard up, as you will find out shortly.

Ezekiel 33:2-6: "Son of man, speak to the children of thy people, and say unto them, When I bring the sword upon a land, if the people of the land take a man of their coasts, and set him for their watchman: If when he seeth the sword come upon the land, he blow the trumpet, and warn the people; Then whosoever heareth the sound of the trumpet, and taketh not warning; if the sword come, and take him away, his blood shall be upon his own head. He heard the sound of the trumpet, and took not warning; his blood shall be upon him. But he that taketh warning shall deliver his soul. But if the watchman see the sword come, and blow not the trumpet, and the people be not warned; if the sword come, and take *any* person from among them, he is taken away in his iniquity; but his blood will I require at the watchman's hand."

Back in the day, there were no satellites. There wasn't cable television to find out what your enemies were doing.

Back in the day, there were no satellites. There wasn't cable television to find out what your enemies were doing. There were no drones to send over their countries. So what you did was choose watchmen to stand up on the wall that was built around your city. That wall was to protect the inhabitants inside, but you still had to know if the enemy was coming and wanting a battle. So, you chose watchmen to stand up there and to look out in the distance. This was a very important job. Why? Done incorrectly, it could cost the whole city its life. That being true, what qualities would you want a watchman to have? Think about it for a second. Remember that if this watchman messes up, you and your family might wind up dead.

A watchman needs to be a person of integrity; someone who is trustworthy; someone who is not lazy; someone who is alert and attentive; someone dependable; someone with good eyesight; someone who cares about people; someone who is not overly concerned what others think about him when he blows the trumpet; someone who knows how to play the trumpet! We don't need someone up there who is just practicing how to play that trumpet, but knows how to make the right sound with it! Someone who is honest. Someone who is principled. Someone who is honorable.

Let's stop for just a second. If your city built a wall around it to protect it from the enemy, and they were choosing a watchman to stand on that wall to protect the people, would they choose you? Do you fit the list in the above paragraph? If not, why not? Are you a follower of Jesus Christ? If so, then all of those qualities should be part of your life. If they are not, today is a new day. Repent for getting off track, and get back on the narrow road. Who you are as you follow Jesus is so very important.

But now watch and see where this section of Scripture we've been reading takes a whole new turn:

Ezekiel 33:7-11: "So thou, O son of man, I have set thee a watchman unto the house of Israel; therefore thou shalt hear the word at my mouth, and warn them from me. When I say unto the wicked, O wicked *man*, thou shalt surely die; if thou dost not speak to warn the wicked from his way, that wicked *man* shall die in his iniquity; but his blood will I require at thine hand. Nevertheless, if thou warn the wicked of his way to turn from it; if he do not turn from his way, he shall die in his iniquity; but thou hast delivered thy soul. Therefore, O thou son of man, speak unto the house of Israel; Thus ye speak, saying, If our transgressions and our sins *be* upon us, and we pine away in them, how should we then live? Say unto them, *As* I live, saith the Lord GOD, I have no pleasure in the death of the wicked; but that the wicked turn from his way and live: turn ye, turn ye from your evil ways; for why will ye die, O house of Israel?"

It wasn't a good day for God when Adolph Hitler died and went to hell. It wasn't what he was created for.

You see there is a loving God out there that does not take pleasure in the death of the wicked. It was not a good day for God when Adolph Hitler died and went to hell. It wasn't what he was created for. It was not a good day for God when Joseph Stalin, Pol Pot, Lenin, Idi Amin, and the like died and went to hell. It wasn't what they were created for. It is not a good day if your hit song was, "I Did It My Way." You find out real quickly when you die that if you didn't do it God's way, you are in a load of trouble.

After famous comedian George Carlin died, I got on YouTube to watch a few clips of his acts. I could not get through one ten-minute clip without him blaspheming the name of God and the name of Jesus. God takes blasphemy very seriously:

> **Leviticus 24:16:** "And he that blasphemeth the name of the LORD, he shall surely be put to death, *and* all the congregation shall certainly stone him: as well the stranger, as he that is born in the land, when he blasphemeth the name *of the LORD*, shall be put to death."

If George Carlin could come back for five seconds to planet earth, it wouldn't be to go on *The Tonight Show with Jay Leno* or *The Late Show with David Letterman*. He wouldn't come back and collect a paycheck for doing a stand-up routine at some arena. He would come back for five simple seconds, repent of his sins, become born again, take his last breath and go be with Jesus for eternity. But it is too late for him. But my real question is, who warned him of the judgment to come? What Christian picked up the trumpet and blew it and warned him that he was going to stand in front of the God that he was mocking?

When Apple cofounder and CEO Steve Jobs died, I did a little research on him. He sold one of his companies for 400 million dollars. He sold another one of his companies for eight billion dollars! But look what Jesus says in Mark 8:36: "For what shall it profit a man, if he shall gain the whole world, and lose his own soul?" Mr. Jobs was into Buddhism. Buddha can't help you the day you stand in front of Jesus. I do know of a man who witnessed to

Remember something very key when it comes to sharing your faith. Sharing your faith isn't a presentation, but a conversation.

Steve. He was the watchman in Steve's life. Steve said no, but that watchman has no blood on his hands. He did his job. It was Steve's job to seek out the truth of Jesus Christ. He chose not to. That was his choice, which now has eternal consequences. But the watchman loved him enough to blow the trumpet.

Before I fly anywhere, I always take time to pray for whomever I will be sitting next to on my flight. One time when I was heading to Newark, I sat next to Darin. He worked for the CIA. So I kept asking him a bunch of questions that he couldn't answer! It was a lot of fun. I was trying to pick his brain, but there were just some things he couldn't tell me. I guess I didn't have a high enough security clearance! I love to learn things and asking questions is one of the best ways to do that.

During our conversation—wait, let's stop right there. Remember something very key when it comes to sharing your faith. Sharing your faith isn't a presentation, but a conversation. This is so important. Jesus had a conversation with the woman at the well, and the rich young ruler. Paul had a conversation with Agrippa and Felix. During those conversations they presented things, but the conversations always went back and forth. Can you have a conversation? As a matter of fact, you do it all

Remember something very simple. The world lies to us all the time.

the time. The real question is: Are you going to leave those conversations in the temporary realm, or are you going to make them eternal conversations?

During my conversation with Darin, he told me that he was an agnostic. Now always remember that if you don't know what a word means, just ask the person: What do you mean by agnostic? What do you mean by atheist? What do you mean by Muslim? What do you mean by evolutionist? Those types of questions keep conversations going, and you can see what the person believes that doesn't line up with the Bible. An agnostic is someone who has not seen enough evidence to push them to believe in God or to push them not to believe in God. That is how most people define it. So I asked, "What would be enough evidence to prove to you that there is a God?" So we started going back and forth. It was a great give and take. He was a smart man with some good questions.

Later in our conversation, Darin told me that he was on Flight 93 on September 11th, 2001! So as I was sitting there, my mind began to whirl. That was the flight that went down in Pennsylvania killing everyone on board. Remember something very simple. The world lies to us all the time. Death to the world means over with: Peter Jennings is dead. Johnny Carson is dead. Elvis Pressley is dead. Michael Jackson is dead. What that means to the world is dead and over with. They are gone. They don't exist anymore. All we have is memories and nothing else. Never forget, that is not what death is in the Bible. Death in the Bible just unlocks the door to the other side! It is just the passing of this life into either heaven or hell. All of those people I just mentioned are either alive in heaven or alive in hell as you read this. Or as I always say, they are either 'alive and well' or 'alive in hell.'

One of the two. But I wonder who warned those people before they died?

Darin then proceeded to tell me that his boss called him on the Friday before September 11th, and said he wanted him in California a day earlier. So he switched his flight from Tuesday, September 11th to Monday, September 10th–still on Flight 93! He then told me that he has his ticket for Flight 93 on September 11th framed on his wall.

So I asked him a very simple question, "Was that luck, was that chance, or was that God that kept you off of that plane flight?" He said, "Yes, yes, yes!" He knew something or Somebody kept him off of that flight! So I let Darin know that the reason that God kept him off of that plane flight was so that he could hear the rest of the story. And the rest of the story is what Jesus did for him on the cross! He told me he liked to read, so I gave him one of my books. You see, my job was simple: to pull the trumpet out, blow the trumpet, and warn Darin trouble was coming for all of eternity if he did not repent and believe upon Jesus Christ for the forgiveness of his sins.

In the Atlanta airport one day, I saw a guy looking at some books in one of the bookstores. He was wearing a black shirt with some interesting designs on it. He had his back to me, so I tapped him on the shoulder. I tap people all the time! It is a good way to get into a conversation, but it also might get me punched one day! As he turned around toward me, I noticed he was wearing a necklace of a pentagram. Now a very easy way to get into a conversation with someone is by talking about what they are wearing. T-shirts, necklaces, tattoos, and rubber bracelets are all great ways to strike up conversations. So I asked him if he was into Wicca, since he was wearing that pentagram. He said, "No, Satanism." Wow! Not the response I was expecting. So I said, "Have you ever read the satanic bible?" He said twice, front to back. Now think about that. I meet Christians all the time who tell me that they have not read the Holy Bible front to back once, and here is a Satanist who has studied his faith more than some Christians have. How sad. Alex and I had an interesting conversation, because I reminded him that what we know about Satan came from the Bible, so if he believed in Satan, he might as well believe in God! He listened to the blowing of the trumpet.

Finally, I got someone to invite me to Hawaii to speak! It sure took long enough, but recently I got the great opportunity to speak there for a week. They wouldn't let me fly in coach. They said I had to fly first class, since it was my first time going to the state, and it was such a long flight. I love people like that! So as I sat down on the plane, there was an older gentleman sitting next to me. I said, "Hello my name is Mark. What is yours?" He said, "Dr. Will." I said, "Dr. Will, I have a question for you: How did you get lucky enough to sit next to me for the next 11 hours?" It was so much fun to see that 85-year-old man laugh! As we talked and enjoyed each other's company, he told me he was an atheist.

Alex and I had an interesting conversation, because I reminded him that what we know about Satan came from the Bible, so if he believed in Satan, he might as well believe in God!

But he was very quick to add that his daughter was a very strong Christian lady and mother. I was excited about that, but remember that none of us will get to heaven because our kids love the Lord. And young people also remember that you will not get to heaven one day because your parents are born again believers. Each one of us has to make our own decision.

I kind of figured something happened to Dr. Will along his journey of life, so I asked him about his past. It turns out, he was a soldier during World War II. He was off on a mission when a mortar round hit the chow line on his base, killing a bunch of his buddies. When he came back to the States, his job was to meet the trains that had the dead soldiers on them. He would meet the train, get the brass casket with the orders, and deliver the body to the parents. He also stated that he was supposed to do whatever the parents wanted. Most of them wanted him to stay for the funeral. So he would do that, then go back and get another body and deliver it, over and over. He was 23 at the time. So I asked him, "Do you think all of your past life experience could have an effect on your beliefs today?" And he said, "The more you think about it, it probably does."

A couple of days later, I was having breakfast on the beach in Hawaii, and would you believe it, there came Dr. Will and his wife–who wasn't on our flight–walking down the beach! We had a real blessed time chatting that morning. He has already written me from his home in Kentucky since then, too. I am very glad that I didn't leave that trumpet at home when I took that flight.

There is a movement among teenagers called the 'straight edge movement.' It is a group of young people that don't drink, don't smoke, don't do drugs, and don't sleep around. They have seen all of the devastating consequences that come hand in hand with those lifestyle choices, and they want nothing to do with it. Now the interesting thing is that most of the straight edge students I meet are atheists or agnostics! They don't come to their position by a belief in God, but because they don't want bad consequences in this life.

Some of you may have heard of a television show called *Jersey Shore*. It is filmed up in Seaside Heights, NJ. I was up there recently for a speaking engagement, and afterwards, we walked around the boardwalk getting into conversations with people. I walked up to a group of teens and had a nice talk with them, and found out that a few of them were Straight Edge. Interestingly, some were atheists and some were Buddhists. They were banking on the fact that even if there is a God, they will have been good enough in this life to be right with Him when they die. We will talk about that a little bit later in the book. It was so good to blow the trumpet on that boardwalk and warn those young people about eternity. I ended giving the group some books and gave them some money to have dinner on me that evening. Later that night as I was talking with someone, I looked over my shoulder and one of those teenagers was standing there with a nice cold bottle of water on this warm summer evening. He said, "I wanted to make sure that you had some water for your throat, so that you didn't lose your voice tonight!" What a kind gesture from that young man. He has also emailed me, as he is in search mode trying to figure out his beliefs.

When I was a kid, our family used to vacation at that exact same spot in Seaside Heights! It was so nice to go back there as a man of God with a trumpet in my hand and put it to God's use.

I received an email from a man one day whose wife is in the U.S. Army. He had caught her committing adultery. He was devastated. He had no clue it was happening. He then asked me about a book that I signed for her. I meet a lot of military people in my travels, and I love to talk with them and bless them with my materials. I actually ran into his wife in an airport! When I signed *One Heartbeat Away* for her, I wrote, "The truth shall make you free." The husband told me that it was the perfect thing that could have been written. I had no clue about the adultery, but am glad God took those words and used them as a trumpet in a husband and wife's lives.

Traveling one day, I was sitting next to a Jewish gentleman named John. I love talking with Jewish people. As we were talking, he told me that his 83-year-old mother became a born again Christian! I said, "Stop playing with me!" He said, "No, she really did. She goes to a Bible study in Boca Raton, Fla.!" I was floored. He looked at me and said, "I have so many questions." I said, "Fire away." What a plane flight!! As we were winding up the conversation, he told me that I sounded just like a coworker of his! He said just the night before, he and the gentleman were talking about Jesus and got up and had breakfast and talked some more. Now that is my kind of coworker! He was being a watchman in John's life.

Remember if you're ever blessed to talk to a Jewish person, you can ask them, "Have you heard of the Jewish Riddle?"

> **Proverbs 30:4:** "Who hath ascended up into heaven, or descended? who hath gathered the wind in his fists? who hath bound the waters in a garment? who hath established all the ends of the earth? what *is* his name, and what *is* his son's name, if thou canst tell?"

The Jewish Scriptures talk very clearly about God's Son!

You folks who know me, know that I love to eat! If I could choose any job, I would want to be a Christian sumo wrestler!! I could eat all day, bump bellies with those folks and share the gospel!! So I train for that dream job by eating! On my travels, I wind up at a lot of restaurants. I always pray though that God will lead me to the right

Remember if you're ever blessed to talk to a Jewish person, you can ask them, "Have you heard of the Jewish Riddle?"

restaurant so I can meet the right people. I can eat anywhere, but you can only meet certain people at certain restaurants.

Recently, when I was speaking in Ohio, I decided to venture over to a town known for its liberal mindedness. So I walked the streets and witnessed for a couple of hours. I was then going to choose between two restaurants. I prayed and began to walk towards one of the restaurants and noticed a long line waiting for tables. I knew instantly that couldn't be my restaurant! I am a tad impatient!! So I walked up the street to the other restaurant, and the hostess, who I thought was the owner, seated me at my table. I began to chat with her. She sat at my table four different times to talk about Jesus! It was one of the 'wow' times in life!

The food that I ordered was fantastic. So I asked Suzanne how many people worked in the kitchen. She told me four. I said, "English or Hispanic?" You always want to know things like that so you give people something in their language. I have

"When you were a child, did you grow up in any religious faith, belief or tradition?" He said, "Baptist." I said, "Now that you are older, is it more important to you or less important?"

been at restaurants where everyone in the kitchen was Hispanic. So I always have Spanish gospel tracts, and copies of my books in Spanish. They were all English, so I took four gospel tracts and wrapped a $20 bill around each one. I said, "Can you give these to each of the cooks and kitchen staff and tell them that a customer was very happy and wanted to bless them today, because Jesus said it was more blessed to give than receive?" And off she went.

Two minutes later, this gigantic cook named John came out to my table. He was the head cook and said, "Are you the guy who blessed my people with this?" He was so thankful that someone would recognize them back in the kitchen. I used to work in the food business, so I understand how hard of a job it can be. The other thing is that kitchens usually only hear when something is wrong with someone's food. Remember that we are Christians. We live by a different standard. We should be encouragers and bless people all the days of our lives!

So I said to John, "Can I ask you an interesting question?" He said, "Sure." So I asked him, "When you were a child, did you grow up in any religious faith, belief or tradition?"

He said, "Baptist." I said, "Now that you are older, is it more important to you or less important?" John said, "Less important. I am spiritual now." These are good questions to ask anybody. As we continued to talk, his 'spiritual' answer was just what I thought it would be. He had the 'many different paths to heaven' argument. Believe whatever you want to, but we will all wind up in the same place one day. John then let me know that he had to get back to the kitchen to check on his group. I asked him if he liked to read, and he told me that he did, so I let him know that I was going to go to my car and get a book for him.

When I came back into the restaurant with his book, there was a big crash in the kitchen. Suzanne went to check. When she came back out, I said my good-byes and was off.

When I returned to Atlanta the next day, I had an email from Suzanne! She said that she had to tell me what the big crash was in the kitchen. One of the cooks took the tract booklet that I sent back, and he didn't like it, so he took the $20 and slid it into his pocket. It is kind of easy to figure out what his god is: money!! Then, he took the tract booklet and slung it into the trash can, but as he did that, his feet slipped out from under him and the plate he had in his hands came crashing to the ground. When Suzanne walked back there, he was sitting on the floor pulling glass shards out of his stocking feet! John, the spiritual guy, said, "I think you need to go get that tract booklet out of the trash can!" Even John knew there was something up with that tract booklet! John was blowing the trumpet in that man's life, and he didn't even know it!

I hate when I get bumped up to first class. Okay, a little sarcasm, there! One day, as I was settling into my upgraded first class seat, the guy next to me said, "Oh, I didn't know anyone was going to sit there." He made me feel real welcome! He said that his wife was sitting in coach, and that they had

You never want to push someone to talk about something they are not ready to talk about. When it comes to something very personal or very tragic, it has to be in their time frame to talk about it and not yours.

flown together for 12 years, and that they had always sat next to each other. I thought he was going to ask me to switch seats with his wife, and I was thinking, 'This is no time to be a servant!' But before I could say anything, he said that he had already talked with a man in the back and that he was going to switch seats with him. I was very relieved! But then, I was also intrigued, because I always pray for the person that I sit next to on my flights, and now this man was up and gone.

So then Joe came up to sit next to me, and as we began to chat, I found he was a very nice man. As we were flying, I hadn't found a door to walk through to get things rolling into a spiritual conversation, so I said, "Can I ask you an interesting question?" He said sure. "When you were a kid, were you raised in any religious faith or belief system?" He said, "Yes, Methodist." I said, "Now that you are older is that more important to you or less important?" His response of 'less' had a very definite edge to it. So I decided to say, "Did anything happen to you along the way, Joe, that kind of pushed you away from God?" He said 'yes' with a most definite edge. I had no clue where this was going.

So, I said what I always do in these types of conversations. I said, "If you feel comfortable Joe, can you tell me what happened?" You never want to push someone to talk about something they are not ready to talk about. When it comes to something very personal or very tragic, it has to be in their time frame to talk about it and not yours. That is a good thing I have learned through the years. He put his head down and just began to think. It was that point in the conversation where the silence got very awkward. After a seemingly very long time, he put his head up and said, "Okay." He then began to tell me how a stalker came after his daughter, and they had to get the police involved. He said the stalker then came after his wife. He stated the stalker broke the restraining order and was arrested and put into a juvenile detention center: He was only 17 years old.

One morning, he said that he was awakened at 5:00 AM by a bloodcurdling scream from his daughter. He went running out of the bedroom, and there was the stalker, standing in the middle of his house with a rifle. He had shot through the sliding glass door and come right in.

Think for a second if this happened to you. What would you do with a gunman in your house? Would you freeze? Would you protect your wife and kids? Would you know at that moment that a bullet that hits you in the right place could make your dreams of seeing Jesus face to face for the first time come true that day?

But the man I was chatting with was not a believer. I said, "What did you do?" He told me that he rushed the gunman. The young man shot, hitting him twice in the stomach. He told me that he kept going and tackled the young man. As they were wrestling on the ground, Joe said it was very bloody, and the stalker slipped out of his hands and got away. He let me know that the police captured him down the road.

He then told me that he was lying there on the floor and thought, "Wait a minute. Where is my wife?" He got up, stumbled to the front door, opened it, and his wife was lying face down in the snow, shot and killed. The gunman had been waiting behind a bush when his wife came home at 5:00 AM, shot her, and then proceeded to the back of the house, and broke in.

After Joe told me all of this, he looked at me and said, "I

Even though I knew it was going to be a tough question; even though I knew there was a lot of emotion flowing in this conversation, I was intrigued with what he was going to ask me. He said, "How can there be a God when my wife is dead, and this man is still alive in a prison in Ohio?"

have a question for you." Remember that conversations go both directions. They go back and forth.

Even though I knew it was going to be a tough question; even though I knew there was a lot of emotion flowing in this conversation, I was intrigued with what he was going to ask me. He said, "How can there be a God when my wife is dead, and this man is still alive in a prison in Ohio?" By the way, is that a legitimate question? That is as legitimate as they come. I said, "Joe, do you believe each of us has free will?" He agreed that we did. I then let him know that once God gave us free will, we could use that free will correctly to have a good conversation like we were having, help the poor, love our families, etc., or we could misuse that free will and lie, cheat, steal, rape, and murder. He saw my point. Sometimes we want to blame God for things that are truly not God's fault. Men and women make decisions that can affect people's lives many years later. The real crux of the issue is that Joe misses his wife. Even though it had been many years, the loss was as fresh as if it had happened yesterday as he told the story.

As we continued talking, I said, "Do you like to read?" To this day, I still get eight or nine out of ten people who will say yes to that question. So use that question, and always have some good literature ready that you can hand to them right there. He looked at me and said, "No, I don't!" So, I signed one of my books and gave it to him anyway! I don't give up easily! By the time we landed in Wichita, he was 55 pages into the book. He looked at me and said, "This is really good, and it is answering a lot of my questions." Praise the Lord! He shook my hand twice, thanked me for the conversation and let me know that he hardly ever shares that story. It is just so emotional for him, because every time he tells the story, he has to relive it. I am so glad I was not fixated on reading a newspaper that day or drinking my tea. I am so, so glad that I brought that trumpet with me and sounded it very loudly on that flight!

I know of numerous high school groups that have literally listed every single teacher, student, and administrator in their schools and made sure every one of them has heard the gospel. One group went through their whole school in three months. Another group goes through their whole school each year. Their goal is to make sure that when a student walks across the stage at graduation, they have heard the gospel at least four times from someone in that youth group! Now that is a group of true watchmen. A watchman knows that sometimes, you need to blow the trumpet more than once in someone's life.

Once, I was speaking at a chapel for a professional football team. The team stays at a hotel on Saturday evening, has all of their meetings (including chapel), and then heads over to the game on Sunday. As I was speaking to the team, I asked them a very simple question: "What is the name of the doorman that is in front of your hotel every Saturday that you stay here?" How many people do you think knew the answer to that question? By the way, do you know the name of the janitor at your school or workplace? How about the name of the person who always helps you at the grocery store, or the person working the drive thru window of your favorite fast food restaurant?

Philippians 4:3: "And I intreat thee also, true yokefellow, help those women which laboured with me in the gospel, with Clement also, and *with* other my fellowlabourers, whose names *are* in the book of life."

Revelation 20:15: "And whosoever was not found written in the book of life was cast into the lake of fire."

Remember that people aren't, "Hey you." Learn people's names. Since names are important to God, they should be important to us as well. One thing I do when talking with a server at a restaurant or someone behind the front desk at a hotel is to use their name a couple of times in the first few sentences. Once you repeat it a couple of times, it sticks in your mind much better.

Remember that people aren't, "Hey you." Learn people's names.

By the way, you were correct. Not one of the football players knew the name of the doorman. So I let them know his name was Raman. He was from Nepal. He couldn't believe that both of my books had been translated into the Nepalese language. He was kind of a mix of different religions. I call it the buffet approach of picking and choosing different things to believe in, because it feels good, or you might like it, but it isn't based upon truth. Saturday after Saturday, these men would walk past this gentleman and never blow the trumpet and warn him about the eternal truths of God. It was so sad. But hopefully, those football players took the challenge to step up and be watchmen in the days to come.

> **1 Thessalonians 2:4:** "But as we were allowed of God to be put in trust with the gospel, even so we speak; not as pleasing men, but God, which trieth our hearts."

You have been entrusted with the gospel. You have been entrusted with the eternal truths that everyone needs to know. What are you doing with the gospel God has entrusted to you?

Now look what it says in the book of Ezekiel:

Ezekiel 3:18: "When I say unto the wicked, Thou shalt surely die; and thou givest him not warning, nor speakest to warn the wicked from his wicked way, to save his life; the same wicked *man* shall die in his iniquity; but his blood will I require at thine hand."

It is the same thing that was said again in chapter 33 of Ezekiel! When I was a kid, my mom would tell me things like what time to be home, to do a certain chore, etc. Later in the day, she would ask me about it. I would sometimes tell her that I didn't hear her when she had yelled it down the stairs earlier in the day! That was a lie. But my mom knew her son too well. Sometimes my mom would repeat something to me when she said it. I knew at that point that one, I couldn't lie to her later and say I didn't hear her, and two, what she just said was important. If God is telling us the same thing twice in the same book of the Bible, it is important. We better not forget it. Warning the wicked of impending judgment is a very, very important part of the Christian walk.

One other thing to remember about the watchman is that when he got up on the wall, he had a much better angle to see things. You can see things better from higher up than you ever can at ground level. Have you ever seen coaches in a coach's box at a football game? They are very high up, so they can see what both the offense and defense are doing. They can see so much more than the coaches on the field.

Colossians 3:2: "Set your affection on things above, not on things on the earth."

Watchmen must always be looking from the right perspective. They must see things the way God sees things. The cross is proof that souls matter to God. When a watchman speaks and warns people about eternity, it proves to God that souls matter to the watchman, as well.

Don't ever forget,
you plus the Holy Spirit are
a majority everywhere
you go!

Chapter 2
You Plus

"Since the days of Pentecost, has the whole church ever put aside every other work and waited upon Him for ten days, that the Spirit's power might be manifested? We give too much attention to method and machinery and resources, and too little to the source of power."[3]
–HUDSON TAYLOR

Even though there are some lonely nights and days when you are a watchman, the watchman always knows that he is not, and never will be, alone.

Hebrews 13:5: "...for he hath said, I will never leave thee, nor forsake thee."

Joshua 1:5: "There shall not any man be able to stand before thee all the days of thy life: as I was with Moses, *so* I will be with thee: I will not fail thee, nor forsake thee."

As God was with Moses, He was also going to be with Joshua! There is no one more faithful than the God of the Bible.

Do you remember the great story of David and Goliath in 1 Samuel 17? It was David's passion for God that gave him the passion to challenge the Philistine (Goliath) who was defying the armies of the living God. It was an act against God, and David wasn't going to have any of that.

David refused the battle array of his day, and appeared to have no protection. But he knew Who he served, and he knew the protection that God provided.

1 Samuel 17:44-47: "And the Philistine said to David, Come to me, and I will give thy flesh unto the fowls of the air, and to the beasts of the field. Then said David to the Philistine, Thou comest to me with a sword, and with a spear, and with a shield: but I come to thee in the name of the LORD of hosts, the God of the armies of Israel, whom thou hast defied. This day will the LORD deliver thee into mine hand; and I will smite thee, and take thine head from thee; and I will give the carcases of the host of the Philistines this day unto the fowls of the air, and to the wild beasts of the earth; that all the earth may know that there is a God in Israel. And all this assembly shall know that the LORD saveth not with sword and spear: for the battle *is* the LORD'S, and he will give you into our hands."

Do you hear the passion in David's voice? He knew he was going to win the battle, because He knew whose team he was on! David also knew that the battle is not ours, but it is the Lord's!

One of my favorite things is to hear about students who stand up in a classroom and defend the truths of God amongst their teachers and fellow students.

One of my favorite things is to hear about students who stand up in a classroom and defend the truths of God amongst their teachers and fellow students. To me, there is nothing like that. A student from the Citadel called me one day. Ted was standing up in his science class, in front of his professor and 300 students, defending the God who creates each one of us, and saying that we did not evolve from monkeys. Or as some say, 'from the goo, to the zoo, to you!' He told me that he didn't think that he was getting through to his professor. I reminded Ted not to forget about those other 300 students who might be afraid to raise their hands but were listening to him and seeing a great example of a man of God who stands for eternal truth and nothing less.

I want you watchmen to never forget that you plus the Holy Spirit are a majority anywhere that you go. If you won't forget that, the sky is the limit to what God is going to do through you in the coming days!

In 2 Kings 6, Elisha warned the King of Israel that the King of Syria was advancing on the nation. The King of Syria came to capture Elisha, because God was revealing the king's action to him before he did them.

> **2 Kings 6:14-16:** "Therefore sent he thither horses, and chariots, and a great host: and they came by night, and compassed the city about. And when the servant of the man of God was risen early, and gone forth, behold, an host compassed the city both with horses and chariots. And his servant said unto him, Alas, my master! how shall we do? And he answered, Fear not: for they that *be* with us *are* more than they that *be* with them."

Elisha's servant was afraid, because he saw that the enemy had encircled them and there was no way out. Death was the sure outcome. He must have thought Elisha was a little crazy to be saying, 'Those who are with us are more than those who are with them.' But as you might have guessed, God wasn't done yet!

> **2 Kings 6:17:** "And Elisha prayed, and said, LORD, I pray thee, open his eyes, that he may see. And the LORD opened the eyes of the young man; and he saw: and, behold, the mountain *was* full of horses and chariots of fire round about Elisha."

God allowed Elisha's servant to see into the angelic realm. And when he did, oh my, look at what he saw! He got to see some of the power brokers of God! A mountain full of horses and the flames of fire coming from the chariots showed quite powerfully that there was no way on God's earth that they were outnumbered! No way at all!

During the Olympics here in Atlanta in 1996, I was just beginning my life as a watchman. I was just learning the ropes of witnessing and getting out there and practicing.

There was one street in downtown Atlanta that had a lot of clubs, including House of Blues and others. It was right by Centennial Olympic Park and was the main drag when it came to partying at the Olympics. I stood at the top of this hill, looking down this street and determined to witness for the Lord. The street was covered with people drinking and partying. My feet began moving forward, and I started my journey. I was able to make it all the way to the bottom of the street without witnessing to one single person! Yup, you guessed it. I totally wimped out. I let the fear of man overwhelm me. But I have a determined spirit, and I know Whom I serve! I circled back around and got back to the top of the

Don't ever forget, you plus the Holy Spirit are a majority everywhere you go!

street and began to pray. I prayed for boldness that only the Lord can give. I then ventured back down that street. It took me two and a half hours to get to the bottom of the street! What a tremendous time it was witnessing for the Lord!

One distinct conversation I remember so well was with a group of guys from England. They were drinking and representing their country, and we began to talk. As we finished the conversation, one of the men turned and looked at me with his fist clenched and said, "Charles Darwin!" He was banking his whole eternal life on that we evolved from ape into man, and that there is no God and there is no afterlife. I looked at him, clenched my fist and said, "Jesus Christ!" I have staked my whole earthly life and my whole eternal life on the death, burial, and resurrection of Jesus Christ. That tomb is empty, or it is not. One or the other. Make your choice, and then make your stand. And don't ever forget, you plus the Holy Spirit are a majority everywhere you go!

One of the great men of the Bible is Daniel. He was taken into captivity as a teenager. Please remember this: Don't ever underestimate a teenager under the power of the Holy Spirit!

When a teenager gets fired up to serve the Lord, they make most adults look like fools. They just have this ability to not worry about pleasing people, but doing the Lord's work no matter what the cost.

Daniel fully intended to keep God's law no matter what. He requested vegetables to keep the Law and not be defiled. His heart stayed with Israel and Jerusalem his whole life.

> **Daniel 6:7:** "All the presidents of the kingdom, the governors, and the princes, the counsellors, and the captains, have consulted together to establish a royal statute, and to make a firm decree, that whosoever shall ask a petition of any God or man for thirty days, save of thee, O king, he shall be cast into the den of lions."

Daniel was a man who knew to Whom he answered. He answered to the Most High God and no one else. It was not about keeping decrees with Daniel. It was about doing the right thing. It was doing the God thing no matter what the consequences were. As I always tell people, stand up for what is right and let the chips fall where they may. Quit worrying about the chips. God owns all the chips anyway! If they all get scattered, He can put them all back together nice and neat. That is what He does. He makes things work out when it doesn't seem like they will. I wonder what Daniel is going to do?

> **Daniel 6:10:** "Now when Daniel knew that the writing was signed, he went into his house; and his windows being open in his chamber toward Jerusalem, he kneeled upon his knees three times a day, and prayed, and gave thanks before his God, as he did aforetime."

Not only did Daniel obey God, he made sure his windows were open, so that everyone would know that he was going to obey God! I like this guy!

Of course we know the consequences of this: He was thrown into a lion's den, and God stopped the mouths of the lions. Daniel made a strong stand. Daniel was a man of conviction. Are you?

I was flying out of Newark airport one day, and walked outside the airport. I saw a man who was a shuttle car driver, and asked him how business was with the economy. Mustaffa told me that he was just hanging in there. He told me he was from Egypt, so I asked him if he grew up Muslim, and he told me that he did. I then asked, "Are you teaching that to your children?" He said, "No, I don't want to force it on them." Wow. What an answer. We are talking God here folks. We are talking eternal life. We are talking the most important subject ever discussed, and I meet so many people that say they don't want to share it with their kids, because they might force them to believe something. I usually ask people: Did you teach your kids to brush their teeth? Tie their shoes? Eat vegetables? Why wasn't it a big deal to force those things on them? They usually get the point. Christian parents who are reading this book, make sure you read Deuteronomy 6:4-9. One of the greatest things you can ever do, and I firmly believe one of the main things for which God will judge us, is teaching our kids the truths about God, Jesus, and the Bible.

Did you teach your kids to brush their teeth? Tie their shoes? Eat vegetables? Why wasn't it a big deal to force those things on them?

Mustaffa told me that when he was a child back in Egypt that his parents divorced. It was very hard on him. He stated that no one wanted him, but there was this Christian lady who was just so loving and caring to others, so she adopted him. She had two other sons. Mustaffa looked at me with tears in his eyes and said, "She didn't have two sons, she had three!" All of those memories came flooding back how this Christian lady, who was a woman of conviction, who did the right thing no matter the consequences, just loved him and loved him and loved him! It meant the world to me. He looked at me crying and said, "How do I become a Christian?"

Are you an encourager? Do people like to be around you, because they know you are going to spur them on to do great things for the Lord?

Remember you might be standing in the middle of an airport, but you and the Holy Spirit are a majority anywhere you go!

One of the great ladies in all of Scripture is Queen Esther. Many know of the famous verse in Esther 4:14 "For if thou altogether holdest thy peace at this time, *then* shall there enlargement and deliverance arise to the Jews from another place; but thou and thy father's house shall be destroyed: and who knoweth whether thou art come to the kingdom for such a time as this?" Mordecai was warning Esther. If she didn't stand up for what is right that was her choice, but God was going to protect the Jews no matter what.

> **Esther 2:15:** "Now when the turn of Esther, the daughter of Abihail the uncle of Mordecai, who had taken her for his daughter, was come to go in unto the king, she required nothing but what Hegai the king's chamberlain, the keeper of the women, appointed. And Esther obtained favour in the sight of all them that looked upon her."

Mordecai was an encourager in Esther's life. Are you an encourager? Do people like to be around you, because they know you are going to spur them on to do great things for the Lord?

To approach the king without being summoned was potentially life threatening. But watchmen always must be more concerned about doing what is right rather than worrying what the consequences might be. Esther laid it all on the line. She prayed and fasted, and God gave her favor. She made her request to the King, and all of Israel was saved because of her faithfulness!

After speaking at a Christian college one time, a young man came up to me and told me that he was from Africa, and had moved to the States to go to college. When he was at home one day, a kidnapper came into the house and tied up his whole family. He was a teenager at the time. He was lying on the ground tied up. He told me that the kidnapper did not do a good job tying his family up, so he stood up, popped his hands out of the rope, and said, "In the name of Jesus Christ, you are not going to kill my family!" This is my kind of guy! I asked what happened next. He told me that the gunman shot! He said it was a rickety old gun, and the bullet did not come out straight, but hit him in the chest opposite of where his heart was. It was pretty bloody. He said that the gunman got so flustered when he saw all the blood that he dashed out the door and ran away! This young man was a man of conviction. You could still see it in his eyes! He knew what the right thing to do was even if it cost him his life. Very simply, that man plus the Holy Spirit is a majority anywhere he goes!

Stephen of the Bible was a man who did great wonders and miracles amongst the people, because he was full of faith and power. But his stand for Jesus was going to cost him his life.

Acts 7:55-60: "But he, being full of the Holy Ghost, looked up stedfastly into heaven, and saw the glory of God, and Jesus standing on the right hand of God, And said, Behold, I see the heavens opened, and the Son of man standing on the right hand of God. Then they cried out with a loud voice, and stopped their ears, and ran upon him with one accord, And cast *him* out of the city, and stoned *him*: and the witnesses laid down their clothes at a young man's feet, whose name was Saul. And they stoned Stephen, calling upon *God*, and saying, Lord Jesus, receive my spirit. And he kneeled down, and cried with a loud voice, Lord, lay not this sin to their charge. And when he had said this, he fell asleep."

Stephen didn't shrink back. He was testifying alone as he was being stoned, but as we already know, he was not really alone! God allowed him to see Jesus before he took his last breath on earth. Jesus was actually standing to receive him! It may have cost him his life, but that persecution caused the Gospel to spread! *Never forget that unless a seed dies, it produces no fruit.*

Stephen didn't shrink back. He was testifying alone as he was being stoned, but as we already know, he was not really alone! …Jesus was actually standing to receive him!

One day, I had the pleasure of talking to a college student named Annalee. She is a bold woman of the Lord. She was taking a religion class at that time taught by a Baptist preacher. So was he teaching the students that there was one way to heaven or many ways to heaven? Sadly, you may have guessed the right answer: He was teaching that there are many paths to get to heaven. Annalee was brought up properly by her parents. She was grounded in the Word of God. She knew it very well. She would raise her hand in that classroom and come back loving and come back strong. She told me there was this one atheist in her class that continued to mock her, but she didn't care. Her God was worth standing for! As we were talking, I started to give her some more ideas of things to say in class. She started taking notes getting ready for the next battle! Annalee wasn't alone in that classroom. She knew that she plus the Holy Spirit were a majority at that school!

For you folks who are now understanding that you plus the Holy Spirit is a majority anywhere you go, check these verses out:

Psalm 34:7: "The angel of the LORD encampeth round about them that fear him, and delivereth them."

Psalm 37:40: "And the LORD shall help them, and deliver them: he shall deliver them from the wicked, and save them, because they trust in him."

Psalm 112:7: "He shall not be afraid of evil tidings: his heart is fixed, trusting in the LORD."

Psalm 118:8: "*It is* better to trust in the LORD than to put confidence in man."

Isaiah 6:8: "Also I heard the voice of the Lord, saying, Whom shall I send, and who will go for us? Then said I, Here *am* I; send me."

Daniel 11:32: "And such as do wickedly against the covenant shall he corrupt by flatteries: but the people that do know their God shall be strong, and do *exploits*."

John 15:5: "I am the vine, ye *are* the branches: He that abideth in me, and I in him, the same bringeth forth much fruit: for without me ye can do nothing."

"One man with courage makes a majority."[4]
—PRESIDENT ANDREW JACKSON

The truth of the matter is that you plus the Holy Spirit is a majority anywhere you go, because He will embolden you with all of the courage that you need!

Psalm 37:5: Commit thy way unto the LORD; trust also in him; and he shall bring *it* to pass.

Psalm 118:6: The LORD *is* on my side; I will not fear: what can man do unto me?

You have to understand that God is not in the business of leaving His people. He doesn't forsake us. He is right with us along the whole journey of life. Or better yet, we should say, we are walking right along with Him on the journey of

life! He cares too much about each one of us to desert us at the time of need. We may not understand what is going on, but He is more than faithful.

A watchman always knows that he is not alone on this adventure. A watchman knows which side he has chosen.

A watchman always knows that he is not alone on this adventure. A watchman knows which side he has chosen. A watchman knows that he can make his stand for the Lord, and the Lord will never leave him nor forsake him. Are you the type of watchman that has that much trust in the Lord? A watchman always knows that you plus the Holy Spirit is an unstoppable force anywhere you go!

In all four gospels
and in the
book of Acts,
more than

of the
witnessing encounters
occurred between
total strangers!

Chapter 3
Hey Stranger!

"You could not be saved through any effort of your own, but now
that you are saved it is necessary for you to put forward
every effort you can to glorify Him."[5]
–Harry A. Ironside

One thing a watchman knows is the importance of testing things to determine whether they are Biblical. We can't go with our feelings. We can't go with what we think might be effective. We have to go with God's truth and nothing else really matters.

This is a quote from a famous pastor: "If we were able to rewrite the script for the reputation of Christianity, I think we would put the emphasis on developing relationships with non-believers, serving them, loving them, and making them feel accepted, only then would we earn the right to share the gospel."[6] There is only one problem with what he said: It isn't Biblical! It sounds good, but you won't find it in the Bible. You don't 'earn' the right to share your faith; you have the right to share your faith. You have been commanded by God to be bold for His Son!

Acts 1:8: "But ye shall receive power, after that the Holy Ghost is come upon you: and ye shall be witnesses unto me both in Jerusalem, and in all Judaea, and in Samaria, and unto the uttermost part of the earth."

It is a command of God to open up your mouth and reach the lost. If you are not doing that, you are disobeying God. It is really that simple.

I have heard people talk about 'friendship evangelism' so many times: 'Let's make friends with someone first, and then we can share the gospel with them.' Ask a simple question: How many times does 'friendship evangelism' appear in the Bible? The answer is zero! You will never see it in Scripture. Now we are supposed to love on people and treat them the same way we want to be treated, but that is not a prerequisite to share the gospel.

We are supposed to do good works. But how can someone know to glorify the God in Heaven because of our actions, unless they know He is the God that we serve?

Matthew 5:16: "Let your light so shine before men, that they may see your good works, and glorify your Father which is in heaven."

We are supposed to do good works. But how can someone know to glorify the God in Heaven because of our actions, unless they know He is the God that we serve? They can see us do good works, but Who would they know to glorify? That means we must tell them about the God in Whom we believe, then they see our good deeds, and then they give God the glory!

I met some atheists that went to New Orleans to help people after Hurricane Katrina. They saw the devastation, and they wanted to do something to help. So now should I assume that people in New Orleans are all going to become atheists, because some atheists helped them out? Of course not. People don't 'catch' atheism by osmosis. Atheists share their beliefs with others and try to convince others there is no God. Lost people don't 'catch' Christianity by osmosis either. They accept it because we are out sharing our faith with a lost and dying world. That is what watchmen do.

Another thing to think about is how long do you have to be friends with someone before you share the Gospel with them?

How do you figure out when it is time? How long will it take you to talk about the most important thing in your life with your new friend? Two weeks? Six months? A year? But maybe that is the real issue. Maybe Jesus isn't the most important thing in your life. We talk about the new baby that was born. We talk about what we got as a birthday gift. We talk about the big touchdown we scored on Friday night. But we are going to wait awhile to tell our friends about Jesus? Something doesn't seem right there.

Also think about your life and what you do every day, every week, and every month. Would you consider yourself busy? If your answer is yes, then ask yourself this question: How many new friends can you add to your life? See if you can come up with a number.

I was speaking at a men's retreat in California, and I actually asked them that question: How many new friends can you add to your life with the schedule you currently have? When I ask that question, the highest I think I have ever gotten is five. Most of the time it is one or two. One man raised his hand and said: "Zero. My job is keeping me so busy, and when I am not working, I want to spend time with my wife and kids!" What a joy to hear a man of God who wanted to spend time with his family! My kind of guy!

But what about all of these servers, gas station attendants, coffee shop baristas, flight attendants, people that sit next to us on flights, drive thru window employees, people in line at the grocery store, etc.? What are we going to do about those people? Since we don't have time to make friends with them, are we just going to let them go off into hell and do nothing about it? Don't we care enough about their soul to strike up a conversation or hand them a gospel tract?

And by the way, have you ever thought about it from a lost person's perspective? Did you ever think that lost people like talking to strangers? Why would that be? Because they can tell

In all four Gospels and in the book of Acts, more than 80% of the witnessing encounters occurred between total strangers! Yes, that is correct. No one had to make friends first.

a stranger anything (and I do mean anything!) because they know they will probably never see that person again. I have had people tell me things that I know for a fact they would not or could not tell a close friend. They wouldn't want them to know that piece of information. But there was a comfort zone for them in telling a stranger. I truly believe God designed it that way.

And never forget, every friend you have today began as a total stranger! If you are married, your spouse used to be a complete total stranger! And aren't you so glad one of you broke the ice and talked to the other person, because it led to marriage. So what it should really all come down to is that we do want to talk to strangers to share the gospel. Some of those strangers might even become your friend one day, and of course, the real key is that we want them to become eternal friends one day!

I have seen a few different studies that relayed some very important information in the Bible. One stated that in all four Gospels and in the book of Acts, more than 80% of the witnessing encounters occurred between total strangers! Yes, that is correct. No one had to make friends first. They met someone, and before you know it, the conversation became spiritual and was not left at just a temporary one.

When people tell me they have to make friends with someone first before they share the gospel with them, my response is, 'No you don't!' It is a choice that we make. And it is usually because we are scared about the consequences. We might get laughed at. We might get ridiculed. Someone might tell the teacher. But as watchmen, consequences are not be at the forefront of our minds. Only obeying Jesus is.

John 4:6,7: "Now Jacob's well was there. Jesus therefore, being wearied with *his* journey, sat thus on the well: *and* it was about the sixth hour. There cometh a woman of Samaria to draw water: Jesus saith unto her, Give me to drink."

Here we see Jesus start up a conversation with the woman at the well. I am sure He was thirsty, and thinking about the long day He had. He probably didn't want to bother her, as she might have been busy. He definitely didn't want to talk about spiritual things, because He might offend her, and then she would go to hell #2 instead of hell #1. What if the disciples came by and saw Him witnessing, and He hadn't made friends with her first? Do you think any of those things were passing through the mind of our Lord? Thank goodness not! He saw a woman in need. He saw a woman hurting spiritually. And you know what He was going to do? He was going to do something about it! He had the answer that she had been looking for her whole life: Him!

John 4:14: "But whosoever drinketh of the water that I shall give him shall never thirst; but the water that I shall give him shall be in him a well of water springing up into everlasting life."

When Jesus met someone, everlasting life was the most important part of the conversation for Him. How about when you meet someone?

Do you remember the story of Philip and the Ethiopian eunuch? Remember that the Holy Spirit directed Philip to the chariot to talk with the eunuch. But do you remember what happened at the end of the account after the eunuch got saved?

Acts 8:39,40: "And when they were come up out of the water, the Spirit of the Lord caught away Philip, that the eunuch saw him no more: and he went on his way rejoicing. But Philip was found at Azotus: and passing through he preached in all the cities, till he came to Caesarea."

Philip didn't even do any follow up! How dare he! I have people tell me that they will not witness to people if they cannot do any follow up. Remember what we said earlier. We do things that are Biblical. We don't make up the rules as we go. And not only did Philip not do any follow up, he was carried away into other cities to preach the gospel to more total strangers!

If someone needs a Bible, I will take them into a store in the mall and buy them one. ... I do as much as I can. But a lot of the time, I can do nothing, and yet that doesn't stop me from witnessing to them.

When I am witnessing, I do as much follow up as possible as a rule of thumb. If someone needs a Bible, I will take them into a store in the mall and buy them one. If they need a local church, and I am from that area, I will recommend one. So I do as much as I can. But a lot of the time, I can do nothing, and yet that doesn't stop me from witnessing to them.

At the grocery store one night, I struck up a conversation with a Christian woman from Ethiopia. I wonder how she became a Christian. Well, there was a eunuch who met a guy named Philip, went back to Ethiopia with his Bible and the Holy Spirit, and to this day we still have Christians in that country! I am so thankful that Philip decided to follow the lead of the Holy Spirit and talk to a complete total stranger that day!

Recently, I received two very similar emails. They were both from people that I witnessed to four years ago. They told me that I chatted with them and gave them one of my books. Now remember these are two different people from two different cities. Yet they had both just read the book four years later! My first thought was, what took so long?! But they both told me it got them thinking, they started studying the Bible, and they both had become born again! Praise the Lord! The really interesting thing is that I don't remember either of these two guys. All I know is that I am glad I took the time to witness to those strangers wherever we were when we crossed paths.

Once when I was leaving a speaking engagement in Tennessee and driving to Alabama for the next event, a heavy downpour started, and I prayed that God would lead me to stop at the right place to pick up some food to eat along the way. I pulled up to Burger King and placed my order. When I got to the window, I began chatting with the young man who took my money. He was a Christian with a pretty strong faith for his age. So I blessed him with one of my books and encouraged him. I then said, "What is the total for the car behind me?" He told me, and I paid their bill for them. It was only four dollars and change. I got off easy this time! I actually do this a lot. It is fun to see people's expression when you bless them. So I handed him another book and asked if he would give it to them and tell them a Christian man wanted to bless them that day and give them one of his books. The young man said sure, and I drove off for Alabama.

When I got home a few days later, I had an email from the car behind me! The lady said that she only ordered so little food, because she didn't have enough money for both she and her son to have a meal! Wow. She then told me that when the young man told her that a Christian man bought her meal and gave her a book that her young son said, "Mom, don't you think that is a sign from God that we are supposed to go back to church?" It brings tears to my eyes again just writing that. She told me that they are now going back to church and serving the Lord again. I am so glad that I wasn't worried about the fact that I didn't know the people behind me in the drive thru lane, but that I chose to be obedient and bless them nonetheless. Praise the Lord!

Just think about the fact that if you are not talking to total strangers when you get a chance, what you are saying is that it is okay for Jehovah's Witnesses or Mormons to go door to door and share their faith with complete total strangers, but that method is not good enough for you? Let that never be named amongst you.

A professor at Liberty University told me that some Jehovah Witnesses came to his door one day. So he invited them in. He compared John 1:1 in both the KJV and in the Watchtower Society Bible. Jehovah Witnesses believe in both of those translations. KJV says that 'the Word was God.' The Watchtower Bible says, 'the Word was a God.' They change the whole meaning of the verse by adding the 'a' in there. So he pulled out the original Greek text and showed them the 'a' wasn't in there, and that they needed to do some more studying. Then, he sent them on their way. A few weeks later, he said that he got a knock on his door. It was one of those ladies! She had gone back and done some studying and she had repented of her sins and become born again like the Bible says to! I am so glad that professor talked with those strangers!

We were going door to door witnessing one summer with some Fellowship of Christian Athletes camp participants in Kentucky. You should have seen these 400 students take to the streets! It was a sight to behold! Watchmen all across that city doing what the Lord had called us to do. As I was walking from one house to the next, I saw a guy sitting on the back of a pick-up truck. So I went up to him and struck up a conversation. He had a few tattoos, so I said, "Which one is your favorite?" He said the five-pointed star on his hand. As he showed it to me, it was really nothing special. Kind of bland actually. I really wasn't sure why he chose it. So I said, "Why is that one your favorite?" He said, "Oh, it covers up a swastika!" Well he wasn't lying! As I looked a little closer, you could see the swastika underneath the star. I told him that I had seen those before on people in prison who were of the Aryan Brotherhood, which is a white racist group. He said, "Yeah, my Dad is part of that group." Now this is getting interesting. His Dad was serving 40 years in prison. I asked him why he had covered it up. He said that he finally got a job, and he was working with people of different races, and he found out pretty quickly that the color of your skin had nothing to do with whether you are a good worker, fun to be around, etc. What an interesting answer. We had a wonderful talk about Jesus Christ, because this guy could still give up his racist beliefs and die and go to hell. I don't want him to go anywhere near a prison in this lifetime and nowhere near hell for all of eternity.

Many years ago, I was very excited to sign a basketball scholarship with Auburn University. I got the chance to chase my dreams of playing basketball, as well as get a degree. One day on campus, a young man approached me and said his name was Rob Smith with the Fellowship of Christian Athletes. I knew about that group, because some of the football players belonged to it, and they met in the athletic dorm. He invited me to one of their meetings. I said I would come to one, and I like to keep my word, so I showed up at a meeting. I have to be honest: You Christians are strange! You had guitars, and were singing songs about Jesus, and I was sitting in the corner sweating bullets! This was way out of my comfort zone. I had never seen anything like this. I kept looking at my watch waiting for it to be over. I was so excited when it was, and bolted out the door never to return.

Now here is a good lesson. Rob did a good thing inviting me to the meeting. I appreciated it. But that really isn't witnessing. Inviting someone to church isn't witnessing. Witnessing is when you go through the gospel with someone or hand them some material, so they know how to get saved. Remember that from a lost person's perspective, a Christian event like that can be very overwhelming. It was for me. I come from a Catholic background, and had never seen anything like that at the churches I had attended.

One year at Auburn, my roommate was Kim Cardwell. He was a really strong Christian. He would read his Bible. He would pray. I would watch his life. He was one of the managers on the basketball team. He was really a good guy that worked hard and had a good attitude. When he would talk to me about God and Jesus, I would listen.

One day in the dorm, two football players came down to my room. They sat on the end of my bed and told me about sin, salvation, what Jesus had done for us, heaven, hell, etc. Now these two guys weren't strangers, but they really weren't friends either. They were more in the acquaintance category. One guy asked if I had a Bible. I said no. So he put his name in the Bible and gave it to me. I actually began a Bible study with a couple of other guys because I began to get intrigued with the whole concept of God and eternity.

So right now, we have one stranger, one friend, and two acquaintances that have shared Jesus with me.

After moving to Baton Rouge, LA, I went down with a friend to the French Quarter in New Orleans one weekend. There were people handing out material as we walked onto Bourbon Street. Some guy put something right into my hand, and I hate to litter, so I put it in my pocket. When I got back to Baton Rouge that night at about 3:00 AM, I emptied my pockets on top of my dresser, and that little pamphlet came out. It was a gospel tract. I sat on my bed and read it. It had an arrow pointing towards heaven and an arrow pointing towards hell with some Scripture verses on the back. I knew which direction I was going, and it wasn't good.

A while later, I was on a business trip in Los Angeles. Some coworkers and I were on a pier at one of the beaches, and this man walked up to us and asked us, "If you died tonight, are you 100% assured that you would go to heaven?" Well one of my coworkers took the opportunity to curse him up one side and down the other. It was not good. You just don't treat people like that. The man had a great demeanor. He said okay, that he cared about our souls, and for us to have a nice day. Well, I began to watch this guy. He literally walked up to every person and every group on that whole pier! Some were very short conversations. Other times, people would give him a hug. I guessed it was other Christians who were encouraging him. This all got me very intrigued, and I began to read my Bible more.

One night, I was watching television and began to flip channels. I caught this Bible teaching show on a local channel. I love knowledge, and I love to learn, and I began watching this show almost every night when it came on. Sometimes I would sit there with a beer in my hand watching it! Well, one night they presented the gospel so clearly, and I knew this sinning machine needed a Savior, and it was that simple. I knelt down and repented of my sins and became born again! That is the story of how I got started in my walk with Christ, and to this day, it is still the highlight of my life!

A total stranger, a friend, two acquaintances, a gospel tract, another total stranger, and a Christian television show all play roles in my salvation.

So I had a total stranger, a friend, two acquaintances, a gospel tract, another total stranger, and a Christian television show all play roles in my salvation.

In 2007, I spoke at an FCA summer camp in Black Mountain, NC. After a nice long drive up there, it was good to arrive and get out of my car. As I was walking toward one of the buildings, there was a man standing there with a University of Alabama cap on. Now you folks who know sports know that is Auburn's biggest rival. He said he was the FCA director at Alabama. I'm not sure he was telling me the truth, but

I decided to be nice to him anyway! As we talked, he pointed and said, "There is an Auburn guy right there." So this guy came over, and we all started talking. I asked when he graduated, and he said, "1982." I was there then. I said, "What sport did you play?" He said football. The football and basketball players all lived in the same dorm. I said, "What is your name?" He said, "John Gibbons." I said, "Take your hat off." He was wearing a baseball cap, and he took it off. I said, "Can I ask you a question John? Do you remember walking into my dorm room one night and sitting on the end of my bed with Bishop Reeves and telling me about Jesus Christ?" I said, "Do you remember giving me a Bible where you put your name on the inside? Did you know I read that book before I gave it away to someone else years later, and did you know that I got born again and saved?" So years later, God allowed me to meet one of the four guys who witnessed to me at Auburn! I can't even tell you how emotional that day was for me. I had always wondered about those guys. Did they stay the course? Did they veer off and let sin win the battle for them? What happened to them? I ended up writing John a three-page letter thanking him for taking the time to witness to me. The amazing thing is that God allowed me to meet him 25 years after he had shared with me about Jesus Christ! Oh, and by the way, he didn't remember the conversation in the dorm room with me, and that didn't bother me at all. Do you know why? Because that meant that he and Bishop witnessed to so many people

He didn't remember the conversation in the dorm room with me, and that didn't bother me at all. Do you know why? Because that meant that he and Bishop witnessed to so many people that I was just one of many!

that I was just one of many! I am so okay with that. I am glad they weren't overly concerned with what this basketball player was going to say about the conversation, but they knew it was their job to be obedient to the Lord. Remember that you don't know whom you are talking to. It might look like a tall, skinny basketball player, but one day he just might be a preacher of the gospel of our Lord Jesus Christ!

Some people tell me that they think they might do some damage if they go right up and talk with a stranger. Instead, why don't you think what great things God can do with the seed that is about to be planted?

One cold Atlanta day, I was dropping off my suitcase to get fixed. I saw a man come out of a restaurant and just sit in his car. He didn't drive off. So I walked up to his car and tapped on the window! Yes, I am a little crazy sometimes. I said, "Did you get one of these?" And handed him a gospel tract. I then asked, "What are you doing in town?" He said he was down here from Minnesota, because his brother had died. He then said, "I have had so many people die in the past year." Next, I asked him what he thought happened when you die. He said he just didn't know. We had a 30-minute talk on this cold, blustery day. He has called me twice since that day. I am so glad that I wasn't worried about if I would do some damage in Jesse's life, and was more excited about what God could do in his life!

Acts 25:22: "Then Agrippa said unto Festus, I would also hear the man myself. To morrow, said he, thou shalt hear him."

Paul had been arrested for his faith. King Agrippa decided that he wanted to hear what Paul had to say.

Acts 26:1: "Then Agrippa said unto Paul, Thou art permitted to speak for thyself. Then Paul stretched forth the hand, and answered for himself:"

And of course we know how Paul responded: "King Agrippa, you are an amazing king. I know this is the first time that we have met, but I have decided I want to become friends with you. So let's become buddies, and in six months, I have the best piece of news you are ever going to hear in your entire life. Give me a high five king, and I will give you some amazing information in six months!" If you think any of that entered Paul's mind, you don't know the apostle Paul. Keep reading Acts 26, and you will see he boldly proclaimed Jesus Christ to the king! He told King Agrippa about the real King of Kings!

> **Acts 26:26-29:** "For the king knoweth of these things, before whom also I speak freely: for I am persuaded that none of these things are hidden from him; for this thing was not done in a corner. King Agrippa, believest thou the prophets? I know that thou believest. Then Agrippa said unto Paul, Almost thou persuadest me to be a Christian. And Paul said, I would to God, that not only thou, but also all that hear me this day, were both almost, and altogether such as I am, except these bonds."

You see, Paul wanted the king to become born again and not just him, but all that were in hearing distance as he spoke. Do you have the desire to see all people come to a saving knowledge of the Lord Jesus Christ? If you do, it won't matter if it is a friend or stranger in front of you. You will tell them the good news of what the Lord has done for them!

One of my buddies is an Air Force Colonel. One thing he does is put one of my books in his flight suit each day. He will then go about his business for the day, but as he does, he strikes up conversations with people and steers them in an eternal direction. He prays at the start of the day that God will lead him to who gets that particular book. He told me that one day, he was doing some parachute training, got into a chat with his trainee and gave him the book. Six months later, he was doing some more training and the guy that was helping him with his parachute pack said, "Thanks for giving me that book. It was perfect timing." Jon couldn't remember meeting the guy, so he said, "Tell me about it." That is a good statement. It gets the other person talking and keeps things conversational, so you're not just giving a presentation. The guy told the Colonel there wasn't enough time to tell the whole story, so they set up a time to meet up and talk more. I am so glad that Colonel takes time to talk to strangers during his days!

"Tell me about it." That is a good statement. It gets the other person talking.

I always love to sit next to college professors on flights! I don't know why, but we always end up having interesting conversations. One professor I sat next to was an atheist. He owned three homes around the world, and taught at one college in Texas and another in South Africa. We talked about God the whole flight. At the end of the flight, he told me that he was a preacher's kid! He said, "I haven't had a talk like this on the topic of God in 30 years! Thank you very much." I am so glad that I didn't wimp out and fail to talk with that stranger.

One time, I spoke at Purdue University to an audience of 6,000 people! Yes, I was nervous. I get nervous before most of my talks, but especially with that large of a crowd. Sometimes when I am nervous, I start pacing, and in this case, I ended up pacing to where the stage director who orchestrates everything behind the scenes was standing. So we started talking, and it turned out that Hal was an atheist. Hal had an earpiece in, and was listening to what was happening and talking with me at the same time. But all of the sudden, in the middle of our conversation, he looks at me and says, "You're up!" But before I walked out on stage, I looked at Hal and said, "Don't go anywhere. I will be right back!" The audience had no clue during the hour that I spoke that I was right in the middle of a conversation with an atheist! When I finished my talk, I walked off the stage, and right over to Hal and picked up the conversation where we left off an hour earlier!

One college student told me she was into friendship evangelism. So I asked about someone that was currently in her life. Did she share her faith at the six-month mark? She said no. At the one-year mark? She said no. Folks, how long are you going to wait to share the most important Person in your life with someone? People can be here one moment, and gone just like that.

One time as I was flying out of Cincinnati, I started chatting with the gentleman seated next to me. I asked him about his accent, and he said he was from New York City. So I asked, "How did 9/11 affect you?" Well, Lance told me that he was in the first World Trade Center building when it got hit! He was in the foyer when the plane hit up top. He had this amazing story to tell me of what happened that day. He then said during the conversation, "I have been searching for seven and a half years now to find out what happens when I die. I have searched Buddhism, Hinduism, and reincarnation. I must find out what happens when I die." So do you think I should have become friends with Lance first, bought a house next to his in Charleston, SC, and then waited six months to talk with him? Instead, I responded to him, "Lance, let me tell you why God put me on the plane next to you today."

> **Revelation 20:11-15:** "And I saw a great white throne, and him that sat on it, from whose face the earth and the heaven fled away; and there was found no place for them. And I saw the dead, small and great, stand before God; and the books were opened: and another book was opened, which is *the book* of life: and the dead were judged out of those things which were written in the books, according to their works. And the sea gave up the dead which were in it; and death and hell delivered up the dead which were in them: and they were judged every man according to their works. And death and hell were cast into the lake of fire. This is the second death. And whosoever was not found written in the book of life was cast into the lake of fire."

When both small and great stand before God, some of those will be your family, some of those will be your friends, and some of those will be strangers you talked to or passed by during your lifetime.

Remember that none of the excuses that we come up with for why we are not being watchmen will work on Judgment Day. As a matter of fact, we don't want any excuses on that day!

Exodus 40:16: "Thus did Moses: according to all that the LORD commanded him, so did he."

What does a watchman do? He does what the Lord commands. And what does the Lord command?

Mark 16:15: "And he said unto them, Go ye into all the world, and preach the gospel to every creature."

He commands that we share the gospel with every person. Not some. Not the ones I feel comfortable talking to. Not the ones that look just like me. 'Go' means get up and do not stay. And since all people need the gospel, we should be talking with all people whether they are friends or strangers.

A watchman knows being a watchman is a huge responsibility. When it is time to blow the

He commands that we share the gospel with every person. Not some. Not the ones I feel comfortable talking to. Not the ones that look just like me.

trumpet and get ready for battle, he wakes up both his friends and strangers in the city to get ready for the clash ahead. The watchman knows he can't win the upcoming engagement unless everyone is ready to go. Let's get many strangers ready for the marriage supper of the Lamb that is fast approaching!

Remember that when you walk out of your comfort zone, you are walking right into God's comfort zone!

Chapter 4
Speak with Boldness!

"The Great Commission is not an option to be considered;
it is a command to be obeyed."[7]
–HUDSON TAYLOR

As you study the Scriptures, you should pay close attention to the words of Jesus. He didn't mince words. He told it like it was. He knew that His Father's business of reaching lost souls was way too important to risk being unclear when He spoke.

> **Matthew 4:19:** "And he saith unto them, Follow me, and I will make you fishers of men."

Did you notice what Jesus doesn't say? He doesn't say: 'Come follow Me, and I will make you a great athlete.' He doesn't say, 'Come follow Me, and I will make you a great student.' He doesn't say, 'Come follow Me, and I will make you a millionaire.' He doesn't say, 'Come follow me, and I will make sure all of your kids are healthy.' He says nothing of the sort. Why? Because He is trying to tell us something. He is trying to tell us that when you repent of your sins and become born again, it is now time to go out and reach the lost. We fish for men. We fish for souls. That is what a Christian does.

As one guy said to me, "If you're not fishing, you're not following!" I will never forget those words. That man knew what being a watchman was all about.

Many times I will ask Christians, 'When was the last time that you shared your faith with a lost person?" The answers are stunning. Many people look at me dumbfounded. Nothing comes to their mind.

Once I was speaking at a church in Texas the Sunday after the University of Texas football team played in the National

Never forget that the cross is absolute proof that souls matter to God. And if that cross is important enough for Jesus to die on, then it is important enough for us to share with the lost.

Championship. I asked the church, "How many of you took the time to tell a lost person about Jesus in the past week?" Fewer than ten hands went up. Sadly, that was a lot compared to other churches that I have been to.

I then asked them, "How many of you watched the National Championship game on television the other night?" How many hands do you think went up? Remember we are talking Texas here! They love their football in Texas. You guessed it: I had a hard time finding anyone without a hand up. So I said to them, "Watching a football game was more important than reaching lost people this week?" As you can tell, I have a great way of making friends!! Actually, they liked the challenge. One of those events mattered for eternity, and one of them didn't. They knew they had gotten off track, and it was time to get back on track.

Many times I will ask people if they know who won the NCAA basketball title five years ago. They have no clue. But then I ask them if they watched any of the games when they happened, and they always tell me sure. So we watch all those games, print out the brackets and write down the teams we think will win. Many people even bet on the games, but we can't even remember who won them five years later! If you can't remember something five years later, it can't be all that important. Do you remember your spouse's name? You better! Do you still know your kids' names? Of course. Never forget that the cross is absolute proof that souls matter to God. And if that cross is important enough for Jesus to die on, then it is important enough for us to share with the lost.

Once when I was speaking at a church in Reno, NV, I stayed with this older couple. On Sunday evenings, the church had small groups in various people's homes, so when the couple came home from their group that night, they told me that the consensus of the group was that I had 'stepped on a lot of people's toes that morning!' I said, "Me?" I know I do, so it didn't surprise me. But very humbly the wife said, "And we needed our toes stepped on." They had gotten off the right path. They live in a great city to reach the lost, and they needed to be challenged to do so. And they were humble enough to hear from our Lord and to do something about it.

So let's see how we can have that fire and destroy anything that holds us back from being watchmen everywhere we go.

Want To:

One of the main things that we must have as we serve God is a desire to do so. It is a drive that takes us out of our comfort zone. Always remember that when you walk out of your comfort zone, you are walking right into God's comfort zone! He owns the land you are about to go witnessing on. The people you are going to talk with? He made them as well. They are stamped 'Made in His image,' they just don't know it yet. They need truth. And it is your job to bring it to them.

> **Matthew 28:19, 20:** "Go ye therefore, and teach all nations, baptizing them in the name of the Father, and of the Son, and of the Holy Ghost: Teaching them to observe all things whatsoever I have commanded you: and, lo, I am with you always, *even* unto the end of the world. Amen."

Jesus is speaking again. Obey Him. The word 'teach' means to instruct. We instruct people by giving them the truths about their sin and truths about what Jesus has done for them.

> **Mark 6:12:** "And they went out, and preached that men should repent."

Jesus told people that they should repent of their sins. If we want to be like Jesus, we should do the same.

Acts 1:8: "But ye shall receive power, after that the Holy Ghost is come upon you: and ye shall be witnesses unto me both in Jerusalem, and in all Judaea, and in Samaria, and unto the uttermost part of the earth."

The Greek word for 'witness' is also translated 'martyr.'

You have been a witness to what Jesus has done, so now go and tell people. The Greek word for 'witness' is also translated 'martyr.' That is very interesting. When you read about people who are martyred for their faith, what is the number one reason they are martyred? Is it because they were picking up trash or wrapping Christmas gifts at the mall? Of course not. They were martyred because they were proclaiming Jesus to the lost, and one of those lost people murdered them.

Rachel Scott was one of the students who died during the 1999 shooting at Columbine High School. After she had been shot, Eric Harris walked over to her, pulled her head up by her hair and said, "Do you still believe in your God?" She responded, "You know I do." He then turned her head over and executed her. Her father said that he found out that she had witnessed to her killers approximately two weeks earlier! She actually got to share Jesus with the people that were going to murder her. Wow! My kind of watchman!

A friend of mine told me that if you ever read Acts 1:8, you should then flip that reference around and go read Acts 8:1.

Acts 8:1-4: "And Saul was consenting unto his death. And at that time there was a great persecution against the church which was at Jerusalem; and they were all scattered abroad throughout the regions of Judaea and Samaria, except the apostles. And devout men carried

Stephen *to his burial*, and made great lamentation over him. As for Saul, he made havoc of the church, entering into every house, and haling men and women committed *them* to prison. Therefore they that were scattered abroad went every where preaching the word."

You see, persecution is not a bad thing. It causes people to make a decision. Either stand up for Jesus or walk away. So when Saul, who would soon become Paul, was arresting people and having them put into prison, it caused the believers to even be bolder wherever they were scattered. That is what Rachel's life did. It encouraged others to be bold for the Lord. And remember, your life can do that as well!

Afraid To:

What holds you back from being bold for the Lord and talking with everyone you meet about Jesus? The biggest answer I get from people is that they are afraid to, and they have the fear of being rejected.

Acts 4:31-33: "And when they had prayed, the place was shaken where they were assembled together; and they were all filled with the Holy Ghost, and they spake the word of God with boldness. And the multitude of them that believed were of one heart and of one soul: neither said any *of them* that ought of the things which he possessed was his own; but they had all things common. And with great power gave the apostles witness of the resurrection of the Lord Jesus: and great grace was upon them all."

In the Bible, when the Holy Spirit comes upon someone, they speak with boldness. They care about the lost and do something about it. I have people tell me that they are filled with the Holy Spirit, they have the gifts of the spirit, etc., but when I ask them when they last told a lost person about Jesus, they usually can't tell me! Well I am not sure what spirit has filled them, but when the Holy Spirit comes upon someone, they speak with boldness! Their love for God and their love for the lost just pours out of them. Pray to make sure the Holy Spirit of the Bible is doing that in your life.

Luke 6:22, 23: "Blessed are ye, when men shall hate you, and when they shall separate you *from their company*, and shall reproach you, and cast out your name as evil, for the Son of man's sake. Rejoice ye in that day, and leap for joy: for, behold, your reward *is* great in heaven: for in the like manner did their fathers unto the prophets."

Have you ever thought about leaping for joy when you get rejected for sharing your faith? Never forget that they are really rejecting Jesus and not you. And the truth of the matter is that should hurt our hearts a whole lot more.

In the book *One Thing You Can't Do In Heaven*, I used this verse in a chapter called *Winning Winning Winning*. I met a traveling preacher named Sam one day. He was of Egyptian decent. He told me that he went up to his pastor one Sunday and said, 'I can speak in front of thousands, but I am not that good at one-on-one witnessing. Do you have any advice for me?' His pastor handed him my *One Thing* book. He said he went home that Sunday and read the first three chapters. When he finished the third chapter, *Winning Winning Winning*, and he realized what the Bible said about rejection, he put the book down, went to a mall, and shared his faith with a complete stranger for the first time! He told me he witnesses all the time now. He also said that he stole my teaching and teaches it all across the country! I just laughed. I told him it was God's teaching and not mine and asked him to teach it to as many people as he wanted to if it would get them out there witnessing!

Isaiah 51:11-13: "Therefore the redeemed of the LORD shall return, and come with singing unto Zion; and everlasting joy *shall be* upon their head: they shall obtain gladness and joy; *and* sorrow and mourning shall flee away. I, *even* I, *am* he that comforteth you: who *art* thou, that thou shouldest be afraid of a man *that* shall die, and of the son of man *which* shall be made *as* grass; And forgettest the LORD thy maker, that hath stretched forth the heavens, and laid the foundations of the earth; and hast feared continually every day because of the fury of the oppressor, as if he were ready to destroy? and where *is* the fury of the oppressor?"

Have we forgotten Who our God is? Have we forgotten how mighty and powerful He is? Have we forgotten how righteous and holy He is? When we remember who God is, and what His character is, we want to tell people about Him!

One thing I always remind people is not to fear men who are going to die! Death is the great equalizer. Go to a cemetery sometime and look around. Tall or short; rich or

Always let your love of God trump your fear of man.

poor; black, white, Asian or Hispanic; smart or an average thinker: We all end up in a cemetery. The big question is: Where do we go after that?

Always let your love of God trump your fear of man. That is a simple statement that you should let get stuck deep within you. Let your love of God trump your fear of man!

We all have folks that we find it hard to witness to. For me, it is the man in the three-piece suit! I get more rejection from that group. They have made it. They have nice clothes, plenty of money in their pocket, etc. I tried to hand one of those men a tract in the airport one day. He rebuffed me and walked on. I stopped and said, "God, today, I am not going to fear men who are going to die!" I prayed for boldness and kept going. I had a wonderful day of witnessing! Remember to keep things in the proper perspective, and you will be just fine.

How To:

Then the big question that people have many times is 'How do I share my faith? How do I get those conversations started?'

Always get people on their favorite subject. What is that? Themselves! That is always the topic they enjoy talking about.

One of the all-time great accounts in the Bible is the encounter between Jesus and the woman at the well that I mentioned in Chapter 3. You can read about it in John 4:6-30. One of the first things you see there is that Jesus didn't have to make friends first. He starts off in the natural before He swings to the supernatural. He talks about water before He talks about living water. So a good thing to do when you are witnessing is talk with people. To this day, anywhere I go in the world, people still enjoy a good conversation.

I was speaking at a church in Canada one time and taught the youth how to share their faith. So then, we were going to head to the mall and do some witnessing. Some adults said, "This is Canada. People don't just sit there and have a conversation with you." They were implying that people were more closed off there and wouldn't talk about 'deeper' things. I said, "Well, I see it in the Bible. It works everywhere else I go. I think it will work here in Canada!" Here is something you should know about me: I don't take advice about witnessing from people who don't share their faith. I am looking for people who live on the frontlines; people who are out there talking with the lost. I will listen to those people, because they have been tested by the fires of front line evangelism.

So we took the youth and some adults and hit the mall. What a great time! We had prayed that God would have some open hearts at the mall, and He delivered once again! Always remember Who you serve and to Whom you answer!

Remember the best way to keep conversations going and not have them turn into a presentation is to ask questions. When you ask open-ended questions, people will answer them. Always get people on their favorite subject. What is that? Themselves! That is always the topic they enjoy talking about. The longer you chat with someone, the better the chance is you will find a door to walk through to take the conversation down a spiritual road.

Later, in his conversation with the woman at the well, Jesus brings up the subject of her fornication. All I know is when you start talking about someone's sexual sin, things are getting pretty personal! But He was showing her something. She had broken God's Law, the Ten Commandments, and she needed forgiveness.

Jesus then let her know that He was the Messiah that she and all people had been looking for. The story concludes with her telling her whole city about Jesus Christ! That section of Scripture has so much good information you can glean to help you as you share your faith with others.

So now, let's take a look at some good starter questions to get going:

One easy way to get a conversation going is to say, "Can I ask you an interesting question?" I use that all the time. Who doesn't like an interesting question? People like interesting questions and interesting conversations. So have one with them.

"If you die tonight, are you 100 percent sure that you will go to heaven?"

This is a good question to ask if you don't have a lot of time for a conversation. For example, this one works well at a drive thru window, a tollbooth, a cashier, etc.

I was walking out of a hotel one day, and saw a man standing there smoking a cigarette. I handed him a gospel tract as I was heading to my car to go to a speaking event. But I knew deep down I was supposed to do more than just hand him a tract. I was supposed to talk with him. So I did a u-turn and went back. I have done many u-turns in my life. I have even done u-turns in my car to go back and talk with people!

Remember if you pass someone up that you are supposed to talk with, just do a u-turn and go back. You won't regret it and neither will they!

Always remember what God can do with a seed that is not planted. That's right: Nothing! So continue to be seed planters for the Lord in the days to come.

So when I got back over to the guy I said, "Can I ask you an interesting question?" He said, "Sure." When I asked if he died that night if he was one hundred percent sure he would go to heaven, he responded, "Yes." I asked, "How do you know that to be true?" Well the guy starts preaching to me! He had a real strong relationship with Jesus Christ. So I challenged him to be bold in reaching the lost, gave him a book, and started walking away. He said, "Before you go, can I say something to you?" So as I walked back, he let me know that 30 years ago, one of his coworkers asked him the exact same question! He told the guy he wasn't interested. That didn't fluster the Christian man. He just told him if he ever wanted to talk about it, to just let him know. Well three years later, he knocked on the guy's door and asked if he could come in and talk. The guy said to him, "Come on in and have a seat. I know what you want to talk about!" This guy already knew that he wanted to talk about Jesus! The man told me that he told his co-worker that he had thought about the question, 'If you die tonight are you one hundred percent sure you would go to heaven,' every single day for three straight years! Wow!! His co-worker just planted a seed with that man, but you have no clue what God can do with a planted seed! And always remember what God can do with a seed that is not planted. That's right: Nothing! So continue to be seed planters for the Lord in the days to come.

"What do you think happens when you die?"

Now this is one of my favorite questions. It is very open-ended, and you will get all kinds of answers from heaven and hell, heaven and no hell, reincarnation, nothing, unsure, etc. After you hear the person's answer, then just ask, "Why do you believe that?" And you are off and running with a good conversation. Remember to let them defend whatever position they choose.

"Do you ever think about what happens when you die? What makes you think of it? What do you think it is?"

This is a way of rephrasing the previous question, and it will build a little more rapport with the person, and it draws them into the conversation.

When I was speaking at a conference in a hotel in New Jersey once, I noticed this man looking at the books on my book table, so I walked over to him. He was not part of our group. There was a big wedding going on and many of the guests were staying at the hotel. This guy had noticed the flat line symbol on my *One Heartbeat Away* book, and it got him intrigued. So as we were talking, he said, "I have to go meet some people in the bar, but I will come back in 30 minutes." And off he went. Well I have heard that line before! But you know what? Just a short while later, here he came out of the bar to continue the conversation!

So he ended up telling me that he didn't think there is anything after we die. I asked him why he believed that, and he said he was an atheist. I responded, "What is the best piece of evidence you have found that there is no God?" I have found that many atheists have nothing to share as they are basing their beliefs on something else besides evidence. Another good question to ask is, 'How did you become an atheist?' You can ask that for many different belief-systems: 'How did you become a Muslim?' 'How did you become an evolution-ist?' 'How did you become a Christian?' A question like that

Use anything around you to get into a conversation. Something on a person's hat or t-shirt, something you overhear them say, a necklace, tattoo, bracelets, etc., can all be good things to strike up a conversation.

lets you sit back and see where they are coming from. It allows you to gather some more information, so you can figure out where you want to go with the conversation.

Matthew and I had a wonderful talk. He said he loved to read and that he went to the library to check out books on the big bang theory! So I gave him a copy of *One Heartbeat Away*. He then looked at me and said, "Can I say something to you?" I said, "Sure." He said, "When I tell people I am an atheist, I always look at their countenance. People always look down on me. You didn't do that, and I want to thank you for not doing that." Wow! Little did I know that as I was witnessing to him, he was checking my face out to see what my response was going to be when he told me he was an atheist!

Psalm 14:1: "The fool hath said in his heart, *There is* no God…"

The Bible is pretty clear. It is foolish to look at all of the evidence of creation, fulfilled prophecies, and who Jesus is and come to the conclusion that there is no God. But that doesn't mean that we are supposed to treat atheists as fools. It would have shut down the whole conversation with Matthew if I would have had a flippant look on my face when he told me he was an atheist, or if I would have called him a fool. It was a good lesson for me. I am so glad that I handled that situation correctly, because I don't always handle conversations the right way.

Another thing to remember is to use anything around you to get into a conversation. Something on a person's hat or t-shirt, something you overhear them say, a necklace, tattoo, bracelets, etc., can all be good things to strike up a conversation.

Many people now wear those rubber statement bracelets. In talking with people about those bracelets, I have discovered that over half of them have to do with death, so it is an easy transition from there into a spiritual conversation.

I will just ask people, 'What does your bracelet stand for?' I did that once at an Enterprise Car Rental kiosk. The attendant said, "Virginia Tech." I said, "Were you there during the shooting?" He said that he was. I said, "Did you lose any friends?" He let me know that one of his friends had died that day. I said, "Since you have seen death, what do you think happens when you die?" He dropped his head and said, "I don't know. I just don't know." You could tell that it was still an emotional time for him having lost his buddy. So I encouraged him some, challenged him to search it all out, gave him something to read, and blessed him financially. I wanted to make sure that man never forgot the Christian who crossed his path on that day.

Walking towards the luggage carousels at an airport one time, I saw a man wearing a yellow LIVESTRONG bracelet. I walked over to him and said, "Does anyone in your family have cancer?" He said, "My wife." I said, "Did she die?" He told me that she did. I asked how long ago, and he told me five years earlier. This man looked way too young to have lost his wife to cancer five years ago. It kind of threw me off guard for a second. I said, "What do you remember most about her?" He told me that at the end of her life, she was just in so much pain, and she loved it when he would give her a bubble bath. He said it would put a huge smile on her face! Can you feel the love there between a husband and a wife? It was great to hear!

I said, "What reminds you the most of her?" He stated, "The number 103." I have a pretty good memory, but I cannot for the life of me remember why he told me that number was significant. But I do remember how I responded to him. I said,

"I just flew in from Sacramento, and I was reading my Bible. I was reading Psalm 103 which says, 'I as God will remove your sins as far as the east is from the west!'" Jay doesn't get to heaven because his wife died of cancer. He gets to heaven when he repents of his sins and becomes born again. I gave him a gospel tract, and he leaned over and gave me a hug! It was one of my favorite encounters of all time.

"Did you grow up in any religious faith, belief system or tradition as a child? Now that you are older, is that more or less important to you?"

This has recently become one of my favorite questions. It is an easy one to ask, because most people grew up in some sort of religious faith. And the other good thing is that it works for any aged person. Young or old will answer this question.

Another good question to ask during a conversation is: **'Who do you think Jesus is?'** Boy will you get some interesting answers to that one! I had a Buddhist guy, Brian, tell me one day that Jesus never existed! I have heard that a few times, but most people won't tell you that the most influential figure in all of western culture never actually set foot on planet earth. So, I asked him about the historians of that time that wrote about Him. He let me know that all of those historians were wrong! I find it amazing that Brian was able to figure out 2,000 years later that those historians were incorrect! Remember Satan doesn't care how foolish your beliefs and arguments are. All he cares about is that you don't repent and believe upon the Lord Jesus Christ for the forgiveness of your sins.

When you are sharing your faith, you need to talk about sin with that person.

One very, very important thing to remember is when you are sharing your faith, you need to talk about sin with that person. Many people are just fine with you believing in Jesus Christ, but they don't know what really sets Him apart from other religious figures. But when you talk about sin with them, then a Savior makes much more sense. Remember that God demands a perfect blood sacrifice for our sins according to the Scriptures, and only Jesus can provide that. No one or nothing else will do.

So a good question to ask is: *'Would you consider yourself a good person?'*

Proverbs 20:6: "Most men will proclaim every one his own goodness: but a faithful man who can find?"

Most people without any hesitation will tell you that they are a good person. But remember that the Scriptures are very clear.

Romans 3:23: "For all have sinned, and come short of the glory of God;"

Romans 6:23: "For the wages of sin *is* death; but the gift of God *is* eternal life through Jesus Christ our Lord."

Remember that people don't die from car accidents, cancer, a heart attack, or a tsunami. They die because of their sins. Period. That means all of us will be dying one day.

Romans 7:7: "What shall we say then? *Is* the law sin? God forbid. Nay, I had not known sin, but by the law: for I had not known lust, except the law had said, Thou shalt not covet."

Thou shalt not covet is part of the Ten Commandments that are found in both Deuteronomy 5 and Exodus 20.

Galatians 3:24: "Wherefore the law was our schoolmaster *to bring us* unto Christ, that we might be justified by faith."

Do you remember the great story of the rich young ruler?

Luke 18:18-27: "And a certain ruler asked him, saying, Good Master, what shall I do to inherit eternal life? And Jesus said unto him, Why callest thou me good? none is good, save one, *that is*, God. Thou knowest the commandments, Do not commit adultery, Do not kill, Do not steal, Do not bear false witness, Honour thy father and thy mother. And he said, All these have I kept from my youth up. Now when Jesus heard these things, he said unto him, Yet lackest thou one thing: sell all that thou hast, and distribute unto the poor, and thou shalt have treasure in heaven: and come, follow me. And when he heard this, he was very sorrowful: for he was very rich. And when Jesus saw that he was very sorrowful, he said, How hardly shall they that have riches enter into the kingdom of God! For it is easier for a camel to go through a needle's eye, than for a rich man to enter into the kingdom of God. And they that heard *it* said, Who then can be saved? And he said, The things which are impossible with men are possible with God."

Mark 10:18: "And Jesus said unto him, Why callest thou me good? *there is* none good but one, *that is*, God."

Remember, there is none good but God alone. No one fits into the 'good' category.

Remember, there is none good but God alone. No one fits into the 'good' category. How can you show someone that they are not righteous in God's eyes? Just walk them through the Ten Commandments as Jesus is doing here. Now the young man is lying to Jesus. He has not kept all of those commandments since his youth. So Jesus presents him with something else to show him that. When the young man wasn't ready to give up his possessions to follow Him, Jesus was showing the ruler that he had not kept God first in his life, and that he idolized those material possessions more than he loved God. Jesus used that real situation to show the man that he had not kept the commands of God.

I was walking up to a nice hotel here in Atlanta to meet a friend for lunch one day. As I approached the front of the hotel, I looked over to the side, and immediately recognized the man standing there. His name didn't come to me, because

I got nervous for a second, but it was the famous rap artist Kanye West and his posse standing outside the hotel! Well as I always say, you only live once, so I started heading over to them. Now I could feel my heart begin to race for a second. I was excited. I knew this was going to be an interesting encounter. I had no clue how it was going to go or where it was going to go, but I was excited to find out.

That is one reason why I don't role-play with people to help prepare them to witness to people. You miss this dynamic. You miss the nervousness and the excitement. You miss the look on the other person's face. You miss seeing their lip quiver when they struggle for an answer. There is nothing like a live conversation. Oh, and the other reason is that you never see Jesus role-playing with his disciples! He just told them to get up and go and trust God!

So I had some gospel tracts and started handing them out to the guys in Kanye's group. One guy said, "What is that?" I said, "A ticket to heaven." You should have seen the looks on their faces. One guy said, "I need one of those!" So I asked, "Do you believe in heaven?" They responded yes. I said, "Do you believe in hell?" They also said yes. So I began to talk about what hell was like. Kanye looked at me and said, "I just read an article in Newsweek magazine about people who flatlined and went to hell." His eyes got real big as we were talking. So I asked the guys if they knew what it took to make sure they didn't go to hell. They told me they did not, so I began the process of walking them through God's Law.

I asked, "Have you ever told a lie before?" Kanye began to speak for the group and said, "Yes." I responded, "What does that make you?" He said, "A liar." Now he is correct, but a lot of people will say 'a sinner,' 'human,' or something like that. If someone responds that way, I just say, if you murder, you are a murderer. If you rape, you are a rapist. If you lie, you would be what? And usually at that point, they will say liar. And let them say liar. Don't answer it for them unless you can tell they aren't going to answer it. You will see more conviction come on their face as they admit they are a liar.

"Have you ever stolen something," I asked. He responded in the affirmative. I asked, "What does that make you?" He said, "A stealer." Now, that isn't the right word is it? I think that is a football team if I am not mistaken! The correct word is 'thief,' but I didn't correct him, because it must be easier to rhyme with 'stealer' instead of 'thief' for one of his songs!

Next I asked, "Have you ever lusted in your heart?" He said, "Yes." "Jesus said that is the same as committing adultery." Remember that the Lord is checking our insides as well as outsides.

"Have you ever taken the Lord's name in vain?" He said that he had. And never forget that is blasphemy against the Most High God. And He doesn't take His name being blasphemed lightly.

"Have you ever been angry at somebody?" He said, "Of course." "Jesus said that anger without cause is the same as committing murder."

I said, "You just told me by God's standard that you are a liar, thief, blasphemer, adulterer, and murderer. Would you be guilty or not guilty on Judgment Day?"

Always remember to keep pointing people to God and the cross. They have broken God's standards and not mine.

"Does that bother you that you would be going to hell?"

Now is when it gets interesting. Seeing the consequences to your actions is very, very humbling and very convicting. He said, "Guilty."

I said, "Would that mean heaven or hell?" He said, "Hell."

I responded, "Does that bother you that you would be going to hell?" That is a good question to ask.

I am not overly concerned about ruining someone's day when their eternity is about to be ruined. And the truth of the matter is, it is not ruining their day. It is letting the law and truth lead them to the cross!

He said, "It does."

Then I asked, "Do you know what it takes to make sure you don't go to hell?" He responded that he did not. So I began to explain to the group more Biblical truth.

> **Acts 3:19:** "Repent ye therefore, and be converted, that your sins may be blotted out, when the times of refreshing shall come from the presence of the Lord;"

> **Acts 26:20:** "But shewed first unto them of Damascus, and at Jerusalem, and throughout all the coasts of Judaea, and *then* to the Gentiles, that they should repent and turn to God, and do works meet for repentance."

> **Romans 10:9-13:** "That if thou shalt confess with thy mouth the Lord Jesus, and shalt believe in thine heart that God hath raised him from the dead, thou shalt be saved. For with the heart man believeth unto righteousness; and with the mouth confession is made unto salvation. For the scripture saith, Whosoever believeth on him shall not be ashamed. For there is no difference between the Jew and the Greek: for the same Lord over all is rich unto all that call upon him. For whosoever shall call upon the name of the Lord shall be saved."

> **1 Corinthians 15:3-6:** "For I delivered unto you first of all that which I also received, how that Christ died for our sins according to the scriptures; And that he was buried, and that he rose again the third day according to the scriptures: And that he was seen of Cephas, then of the twelve: After that, he was seen of above five hundred brethren at once; of whom the greater part remain unto this present, but some are fallen asleep."

> **Colossians 1:14:** "In whom we have redemption through his blood, *even* the forgiveness of sins:"

I explained to Kanye and his group the simple truths of repenting of your sins and believing upon the Lord Jesus

You have heard the old adage, "Practice makes perfect"? When it comes to witnessing, remember: Practice, Practice, Practice!! Practice doesn't make you perfect, but it does make you prepared.

Christ for the forgiveness of those sins.

Later that day, I got on the internet to find out some more things about the man to whom I had just witnessed. Interestingly, I found something that said he had gotten saved during one stretch in his life after he had a very serious car accident and was going through a tough time. Wait a minute. Think back for a second. Do you remember that he couldn't tell me what it took to get rid of his sins? How could someone be born again and not know that? They can't. That is the issue. He wasn't saved. What you see a lot of people do is make an emotional decision for Jesus Christ when they go through a tough time, and then once they get through the tough time, just go back to their previous lifestyle.

> **Luke 9:62:** "And Jesus said unto him, No man, having put his hand to the plough, and looking back, is fit for the kingdom of God."

When we get saved, we are forward thinking people and not backward thinking people.

Remember that every watchman has a desire to reach the lost. Watchmen know that you cannot be afraid to blow the trumpet. And a watchman will always learn how to talk to the lost. You have heard the old adage, "Practice makes perfect"? When it comes to witnessing, remember: Practice, Practice, Practice!! Practice doesn't make you perfect, but it does make you prepared.

The great baseball player, Albert Pujols once told me that in the offseason, he takes 30,000 practice swings. I said, "No you don't." He said, "Yes, I do." That is a lot of swings! But, he is considered one of the greatest right hand hitters of all time. And once I found out how much he practices, I understand why! All of those practice swings do not make him a perfect hitter. But they do make him a very prepared hitter. Keep practicing, and you will be more and more prepared as you reach the lost.

You see, a watchman knows you only need two things to share your faith and be bold for God: To be born again and to be breathing! If you are saved, and you are still breathing, you are now ready to be a soul winner for the Most High God!!

❖ •NOTICE• ❖

Department of Prayer & Supplication

Our offices are CLOSED.
God is taking some time
off and will be
unavailable to take your
prayers until Sunday
after next. Check back then.
We apologize for any
inconvenience this
may cause.

❖

God is still on His throne.
He doesn't take days off.
We might, but He doesn't.

Chapter 5
Prayer Changes Things

"You must go forward on your knees."[8]
—HUDSON TAYLOR

The words 'pray,' 'prayer,' and 'praying' show up more than 500 times in the Bible.

Romans 1:8-10: "First, I thank my God through Jesus Christ for you all, that your faith is spoken of throughout the whole world. For God is my witness, whom I serve with my spirit in the gospel of his Son, that without ceasing I make mention of you always in my prayers; Making request, if by any means now at length I might have a prosperous journey by the will of God to come unto you."

So let's see what Paul is doing here. His prayer has thanksgiving and praise in it. He is interceding for others. "Prayer is conversation with God (v.9 'my prayers' refers to Paul's intimate relationship with God as a Father and Friend)."[9]

Paul is also asking for things in his prayer. Look at his attitude. He is not demanding things from God. His attitude is one of graciousness. Always remember that our requests must be according to God's will, and we pray in Jesus' name.

Our prayers as watchmen must be for the lost souls out there.

1 Timothy 2:3, 4: "For this *is* good and acceptable in the sight of God our Saviour; Who will have all men to be saved, and to come unto the knowledge of the truth."

And remember also that we should pray for more Christian laborers to reach lost men and women before it is too late.

Matthew 9:37, 38: "Then saith he unto his disciples, The harvest truly *is* plenteous, but the labourers *are* few; Pray ye therefore the Lord of the harvest, that he will send forth labourers into his harvest."

One thing I want you to get stuck way down in your heart is that prayer changes things.

> **2 Corinthians 1:8-11:** "For we would not, brethren, have you ignorant of our trouble which came to us in Asia, that we were pressed out of measure, above strength, insomuch that we despaired even of life: But we had the sentence of death in ourselves, that we should not trust in ourselves, but in God which raiseth the dead: Who delivered us from so great a death, and doth deliver: in whom we trust that he will yet deliver *us*; Ye also helping together by prayer for us, that for the gift *bestowed* upon us by the means of many persons thanks may be given by many on our behalf."

God answers His people's prayers when they line up with His will. It is really that simple. Now it may not be in our time frame or exactly how we want it, but that is why we need to have an unwavering faith in our Lord. We can't see the bigger picture. He might be leaving that person in jail a little bit longer, because He has a much bigger reason going on that we can't see yet. He may not heal that person of sickness and disease. He may let it linger to reach more doctors and nurses for Jesus Christ. He may not answer that prayer for a job right away. He might let you have that time off without the pressures of work to spend more time with your family and to hit the streets to plant seeds with the lost. The real question is will you trust Him during all of those times?

But remember that we can also put God in a position not to hear our prayers.

> **James 4:3:** "Ye ask, and receive not, because ye ask amiss, that ye may consume *it* upon your lusts."

Asking for selfish reasons will not move the heart of God.

> **Isaiah 59:1, 2:** "Behold, the LORD'S hand is not shortened, that it cannot save; neither his ear heavy, that it cannot hear: But your iniquities have separated between you and your God, and your sins have hid *his* face from you, that he will not hear."

Living a sinful life will literally cause God to hide His face from us. Just wrestle with the ramifications of that concept for a second.

> **Isaiah 1:15:** "And when ye spread forth your hands, I will hide mine eyes from you: yea, when ye make many prayers, I will not hear: your hands are full of blood."

God takes how we live this life very seriously. He is not some big vending machine in the sky where we throw up a prayer; pull a lever, and whatever we asked for drops from the heavens. No, He is concerned about our character. He is concerned about our thoughts and emotions, and how we treat people. He is concerned if we are representing Him well in this crazy world.

It is very important as you live this life to have older believers around you. We need people who are farther down the road than us, who love the Lord, live for Him, and are soul winners....

Keep in mind that if you get off track, you can repent and get back on the narrow road:

> **Psalm 32:5:** "I acknowledged my sin unto thee, and mine iniquity have I not hid. I said, I will confess my transgressions unto the LORD; and thou forgavest the iniquity of my sin. Selah."

> **James 4:8:** "Draw nigh to God, and he will draw nigh to you. Cleanse *your* hands, *ye* sinners; and purify *your* hearts, *ye* double minded."

It is very important as you live this life to have older believers around you. We need people who are farther down the road than us, who love the Lord, live for Him, are soul winners, and won't be turning back anytime soon. We can watch them finish their lives well for the Lord. If they haven't walked away from God by this late in their life, the chances are very slim that they ever will.

Saying one thing and doing another will not cut it in the long term as a Christian. It will also hinder your prayers from being answered.

Two of my dearest friends in life are both over 70 years old. They are two men of God that I have the utmost respect for. How they live for God, treat their wives and families, reach the lost, etc., speaks volumes into my life. One of them is Dr. Jobe Martin (www.evolutionofacreationist.com). Almost every time Dr. Martin and I talk on the phone or spend time together, he uses this one verse with me either in conversation or in prayer at the end:

Colossians 1:10: "That ye might walk worthy of the Lord unto all pleasing, being fruitful in every good work, and increasing in the knowledge of God;"

Through his years of following the Lord, Dr. Martin knows how important it is to live your life the right way once you are born again. Saying one thing and doing another will not cut it in the long term as a Christian. It will also hinder your prayers from being answered. As watchmen, we want lives that are pleasing to the Most High God!

I was speaking once at a conference in Rockford, IL, and after the last session on that Saturday, a large group of people went out to eat. It was the weekend right before Thanksgiving, and it was a good time for some fellowship. When we got to the restaurant, they put us at a long table that fit all 30 of us! Before it was time to eat, I asked the host of the conference, "Why don't you pray for all of us?" He responded, "Why don't you pray for all of us?" You see as a watchman, you can't worry about being put on the spot. Actually the 'spot' is where great things can happen for the Lord! I said sure. A little nervously, I stood up and asked our group to quiet down, so we could pray for our meal. So I began to pray. As I did, the entire section of the restaurant got quiet! So I included them in the prayer as well and prayed that their families would have a wonderful holiday as we all have so much for which we should be thankful. I closed the prayer in the name of Jesus Christ, and sat down. Well the room very slowly began to start talking again and everything returned to normal. I looked over at a table and there was this older couple sitting there. They just kept staring and staring at me. So I got up and went and sat at their table! I know. That is a little crazy, but I wanted to find out why they were staring. As we began to talk, I discovered that they grew up in a formal Lutheran church and had never really seen anyone pray like that before. They were intrigued. So we talked about Jesus Christ, and I blessed them with something to read.

At the end of the evening, a waitress walked over to our table. She told me that she wasn't even working in our section, but as I began to pray, she was walking through and stopped to listen. She said, "We hear very few people pray in the name of Jesus in this restaurant." Wow! Another reason to always pray in His name, because that name gets people thinking.

> **Philippians 2:6-11:** "Who, being in the form of God, thought it not robbery to be equal with God: But made himself of no reputation, and took upon him the form of a servant, and was made in the likeness of men: And being found in fashion as a man, he humbled himself, and became obedient unto death, even the death of the cross. Wherefore God also hath highly exalted him, and given him a name which is above every name: That at the name of Jesus every knee should bow, of *things* in heaven, and *things* in earth, and *things* under the earth; And *that* every tongue should confess that Jesus Christ *is* Lord, to the glory of God the Father."

A watchman knows it is Jesus and Jesus alone that will be doing his bidding. He better proclaim His name and His name alone as he blows the trumpet in many people's lives.

Psalm 4:1: "To the chief Musician on Neginoth, A Psalm of David. Hear me when I call, O God of my righteousness: thou hast enlarged me *when I was* in distress; have mercy upon me, and hear my prayer."

Psalm 5:3: "My voice shalt thou hear in the morning, O LORD; in the morning will I direct *my prayer* unto thee, and will look up."

Psalm 39:12: "Hear my prayer, O LORD, and give ear unto my cry; hold not thy peace at my tears: for I *am* a stranger with thee, *and* a sojourner, as all my fathers *were*."

Psalm 64:1: "Hear my voice, O God, in my prayer: preserve my life from fear of the enemy."

Jabez was more honorable than his brothers. He was obedient to God.

Proverbs 15:8: "The sacrifice of the wicked *is* an abomination to the LORD: but the prayer of the upright *is* his delight."

1 Chronicles 4:10: "And Jabez called on the God of Israel, saying, Oh that thou wouldest bless me indeed, and enlarge my coast, and that thine hand might be with me, and that thou wouldest keep *me* from evil, that it may not grieve me! And God granted him that which he requested."

A lot of you will remember when *The Prayer of Jabez* book was all the rage a few years ago. I was witnessing to a Buddhist man at a music festival one time, and he told me that he prayed the prayer of Jabez and it really worked! It was just a mantra to him. But what so many people don't know about the prayer of Jabez is actually what the Bible says in the verse before the prayer:

1 Chronicles 4:9: "And Jabez was more honourable than his brethren: and his mother called his name Jabez, saying, Because I bare him with sorrow."

Jabez was more honorable than his brothers. He was obedient to God. He was trustworthy, and that is one of the reasons God was blessing him. We too many times want God's blessings, but don't want to first make sure our lives line up with His words in the Bible. I pray for favor a lot. But I pray for favor I do not deserve. I deserve hell. This keeps me humble, as I see God give me favor that I do not at all deserve.

"Tragedy does one of two things: It will either drive you directly to God or directly away."

My family goes to the same restaurant each Thanksgiving if my mom doesn't cook. While in the buffet line once, I saw a lady wearing dog tags. So I walked up to her and asked her if her son was in the military. She said yes. I then asked, "Did he die?" She said that he did. I said, "How did that affect your belief in God?" She said, "Tragedy does one of two things: It will either drive you directly to God or directly away." I said, "How did it drive you?" We had the most fascinating talk. She was a mom with a very strong faith in Jesus Christ. She told me that when her son went over to Iraq that he was not saved. She prayed and prayed and prayed for him. She would get letters from him from time to time. The last letter that she got from him let her know that she was not going to see him again. He just knew he would be dying soon. He let his mom know that it would be okay as he had gotten saved and was serving God. The next time she heard about him was when she got a knock on the door that her son had been killed in action. She was a really special lady. It was a real blessing to chat with her and to be reminded that God answers the prayers of moms!

During my travels, I always pray that I will go to the right restaurants. Once as I walked up to a highly recommended restaurant in Iowa, there was this really long line to get in. I am still impatient, so I asked for a different restaurant recommendation, and they suggested a place down the street. There,

I walked right in and was seated. During my meal, the manager came over a couple of times to check on me so I started asking him questions. He told me that as a child, he was molested

at a summer camp. The case ended up going to trial, and he had to go on the witness stand and point out his attacker. He then told me that if he would have come forward about what happened a lot sooner, it might have saved some other boys from going through what he had to go through. So he was living with guilt from that on top of everything else. He then told me that his cur-

One of the things that you miss out on in life if you don't witness is perspective.

rent girlfriend had an eight-year-old son, and one day, her former boyfriend–her son's father–came over to the house and shot and killed the boy! One of the things that you miss out on in life if you don't witness is perspective. When I meet people like Mike that go through all of that, my life is so easy. It is a piece of cake being me. But it also makes me very thankful that I have not had to go down the road he has. Surprisingly, he was very open to the topic of Jesus Christ. I thought there might be anger there, but there was not. That is why I pray to go to the right restaurant, because I couldn't have met Mike at the first place I went. And one year later, when I was in the same city, I went back to the same restaurant and ran into three people that I had seen the previous year! Mike and I got to pick up the conversation from where we left off. We actually just sat at a table and chatted for a while. God is so kind.

In Pittsburgh one Friday afternoon, a friend and I were trying to find a place to eat dinner! Finding a restaurant on a Friday at dinner time near a mall is not an easy task. The first three places we found were loaded with people, but we went to restaurant number four, and thankfully, Johnny Carino's on this night was not too busy. So as we walked in, I started talking with the hostess. We got into a spiritual conversation, and it was very interesting. Then the manager walked over. That can always get interesting when someone walks in halfway through a conversation. Jill was very open and asked some good questions. She said, "My mom would like you." Her mom was a very strong Christian. So I gave her one of my books for her mom. About a week later, I got an email from her mom. She told me that she lives in South Carolina and that she had been praying for someone to witness to her daughter up in Pittsburgh! Well it only took us going to four restaurants to find her daughter, but God is great!

God really started hitting me

Some students told me that they would leave those verses by their bed at night to read. They called it the 'witnessing paragraph!' They said it covered so much of what they need to be doing as they reach the lost.

with the challenge of reaching the lost when I was a Bible teacher at a Christian school in Columbus, GA, so I naturally taught it to my students. Some of them told me that they just loved some verses in Colossians:

> **Colossians 4:2-6:** "Continue in prayer, and watch in the same with thanksgiving; Withal praying also for us, that God would open unto us a door of utterance, to speak the mystery of Christ, for which I am also in bonds: That I may make it manifest, as I ought to speak. Walk in wisdom toward them that are without, redeeming the time. Let your speech *be* always with grace, seasoned with salt, that ye may know how ye ought to answer every man."

Some students told me that they would leave those verses by their bed at night to read. They called it the 'witnessing paragraph!' They said it covered so much of what they need to be doing as they reach the lost. Go back and look at those verses again. They are just loaded with eternal truth when it comes to being a watchman.

When you are out there witnessing, it is always fun to witness in groups. That way, when someone is witnessing, the other folks can be praying and then jump in when necessary. Afterwards, you can debrief about what happened and what you could have done better, and then pray for the person you just spoke with, and for the next encounter. We had a bunch of youth witnessing in Panama City Beach one time, and we broke up into groups of three and four. I had a young man named Allen in my group, and he was just hanging on my hip and watching the encounters. Then during one conversation, he just jumped in and said something that had nothing to do with what we were talking about! Well he was a little nervous, but I loved his boldness. So I let him keep talking and then I pulled the conversation back where I wanted it to be. Within thirty minutes, he was ready to go and walked off to start witnessing. A little later, I turned around and saw him having this great conversation with a police officer! I loved how bold he was and was impressed!

One pastor reminded me that if you pray for divine appointments, whoever is in front of you is that divine appointment! That was a great piece of advice.

When we go out witnessing, we always pray for divine appointments. One pastor reminded me that if you pray for divine appointments, whoever is in front of you is that divine appointment! That was a great piece of advice.

One day, we had some of our students in the mall witnessing, and I saw Spence sit down and start talking with a woman on a bench. He looked like he was doing fine, so I walked off to find someone to talk with. About an hour later, Spence rushed up to me and said, "Mr. Cahill, you wouldn't believe what just happened!" He told me that he asked the woman the question, 'If you die tonight are you one hundred percent assured that you would go to heaven?' He told me that she just put her head down and began to cry. He didn't know what to do. So he told me he just sat there until she began to talk. When she did begin to talk, she let Spence know that her 17-year-old son had died in a car accident one week earlier. And you guessed it: Spence was 17. So you know what she was doing: She was picturing her son. She was a Hindu lady that was very open to hearing about Jesus Christ. Spence was the perfect person to chat with her and even got to give her a hug when they were finished talking.

Computers are great to use, but I think they are going to be the death of me one day! So as my computer broke again, I kept procrastinating taking it to the store to get it fixed. Finally, I walked out the door with it. As I got it out of my car to walk into the store, out walks one of my high school friends, Duane. He looked at me and said, "Funny I should meet you here!" I said, "Why is that?" He pulled his phone out and showed me a text message that he had just sent out to a bunch of his friends the night before. In the message he told his friends that he had just finished reading my book *One Thing You Can't Do In Heaven*, and that if they hadn't read it, they needed to! It was good catching up with Duane, and again, another answer to prayer.

When I leave my house, I open up my door and stand at the threshold. I will usually put my hands up and begin to pray: "Father don't let me be a wimp today. Open my mouth and give me boldness to share about your Son. Move me to the right, move me to the left. Don't let me fear man. Order my steps. Please give me those divine appointments. Protect me as I go. And if you allow me to put my head back on my pillow tonight, show me why I was alive. And please make sure it was for your glory and not mine!" And then I step across the threshold and begin my journey.

I also do the same thing when I am traveling and staying in hotels. I did that one day, and then walked out of my room. Right next to the door was a lady by her cleaning cart. So I struck up a conversation with the maid. She said, "I prayed to God to show me this morning that He was real, and now He has me talking to you!" Trust me, when you are the answer to someone's prayer, it is very, very humbling.

She said, "I prayed to God to show me this morning that He was real, and now He has me talking to you!" Trust me, when you are the answer to someone's prayer, it is very, very humbling.

On a flight to L.A. one time, I was walking up to the front of the plane, and I heard the words "Holy Spirit." I looked over and the flight attendant had the curtain pulled talking with someone. So I decided to butt in. I do that periodically! It is kind of fun. Well I step behind the curtain, and she was praying with a man who was dying from cancer! He was going to L.A. to talk with one more doctor for one more possible cure. He had to be off his pain medication for these tests, and he was really hurting. Both the flight attendant and I got to pray for this man and talk to him about biblical salvation and not trusting a church for your salvation.

In the Cincinnati airport one time, I was walking around looking for someone to witness to before I got on my flight. As I walked by two guys having a conversation, I overheard the word 'apologetics.' So you guessed it: I butted in again! The one man was witnessing to his boss, who he was dropping off at the airport for a trip. He was doing a really good job. I helped him out some, but I loved his boldness. He asked me to wait there a minute while he walked his boss to security, and when he came back, he told me that he had been witnessing to his boss for a long time, but his boss had never wanted anything to do with it.

This gentleman called me once, many months later. He was sitting at his desk at work crying. Why? His boss told him that he never read any of the materials that he had given him, even though he had said he would. It hurt him that his boss had lied to him, but it broke his heart that his boss wanted nothing to do with Jesus Christ. But this man was a watchman, and he had done his job.

Checking my messages one day, I got a voice mail from a gentleman who said he was Clyde Kendall, and that he read one of my books and wanted to meet up for lunch. He was 89-years-old, and he wanted me to respond to him ASAP! Well, I don't do ASAP very well, because most of the time, when people want you to do something as soon as possible, it is because they have messed up on their end, and now want you to rush to help them out. If you think about it, that is very true. In this particular case, I was busy with some things and forgot to call Clyde back.

A few days later, I got another call from Clyde to call him ASAP. I began to think about it. I guess when you are 89-years-old everything is ASAP! So I figured I better call him back! So we chatted on the phone and scheduled a lunch appointment. He wanted to go to Golden Corral. Isn't that where all older people go?! But I told him to pick the restaurant, and I would pay. So as I pulled up to the restaurant, I saw a man standing outside handing gospel tracts to people who were walking in! Yep, it was Clyde. I knew instantly I was going to like this guy!

It turned out that Clyde was a WWII veteran who was actually on a ship that sank. Half of the men on board died. He was also a travelling tent preacher back in the day. One day

The whole time I was talking, this one officer would not make eye contact with me. When I finished, I shook each officer's hand, and when I got to him, he looked up, shook my hand, nodded, and that was it. It was really strange, but my job is to be a watchman...

some heavy winds came through and completely destroyed the tent. This man had an amazing life story. Make sure you are spending time talking to older folks as they have so much to pass down to us younger people.

As we were talking, I noticed some police officers sit down at a nearby table. I like to bless people, so I walked over and struck up a conversation thanking them for their service. I also wanted to bless them with some of my books and DVDs, but had run out, so I went out to the car to get some more. So I brought some back in and began to explain them to the three officers. The whole time I was talking, this one officer would not make eye contact with me. When I finished, I shook each officer's hand, and when I got to him, he looked up, shook my hand, nodded, and that was it. It was really strange, but my job is to be a watchman and bless people. So I went back and finished my lunch with Clyde.

This is an email that I got soon after from Detective Blissitt:

"Mark,

You probably don't remember me, but a couple of weeks ago you gave my partners Det. Munoz, Det. Hutto and I copies of both your books while we were having lunch at the Golden Corral in Jonesboro, GA. My name is Chuck Blissitt, and I'm a homicide detective for the Clayton Co. Police Dept. Please forgive me for my silence on that day, but my job has made me somewhat cautious of people. I've been a cop for 17 years. The past 10 years have been spent working homicide, and I have a hard time with trusting people I don't know. I want you to know that I read both your books, and it has completely changed my life. I accepted Christ as my Savior at an early age, but I have never truly lived my life for Him. I was lukewarm. I can count on one hand the number of times I actually witnessed to someone during the 45 years of my existence on this earth, and I am truly ashamed. After reading *One Thing You Can't Do In Heaven*, it opened my eyes to what is important and that's telling others about Jesus. I found myself going up to complete strangers and witnessing to them. I also witnessed to Det. Munoz who is Catholic and Det. Hutto who I found doesn't really believe

"I can't count the number of bodies I've stood over at crime scenes...I would look at the dead as just objects and not people with a soul. Now, I look at everyone as someone who needs the Lord, and I can't wait to tell others about Him."

in God. Det. Munoz was very receptive to what I had to say, and said that she would read the books you gave her. Mark, I've seen Satan's work first hand, and I'm here to tell you, he is real. I can't count the number of bodies I've stood over at crime scenes, and it just gets worse each day. Over the years, to keep from going insane, I would look at the dead as just objects and not people with a soul. Now, I look at everyone as someone who needs the Lord, and I can't wait to tell others about Him. Mark, thank you from the bottom of my heart for caring enough to speak to us that day and sharing Jesus with us. It really opened my eyes, and I'll never forget you. I've been praying for you ever since and will continue to do so."

Little did I know that day that I was going to meet a watchman named Clyde for lunch, and little did I know I was about to meet another watchman that day by the name of Detective Blissitt! I always remind people that you never know who you are talking with. It might look like an uninterested detective, but he might just be a bold soul winner one day!

After preaching at a church one day in Atlanta, I stopped at a gas station on the way home. Now I always pray to go to the right gas station to meet the right people. This intersection had two gas stations right across from each other. So I pulled into the one I felt I was supposed to go to. As I was walking into the store for the second time (I needed some more materials to give away!), a man came walking out with his Sunday paper. So I walked up to him with a gospel tract and said, "Did you get one of these?" His response, "I'm not interested!" He said it very gruffly. I am guessing he woke up on the wrong side of the bed that morning! My response was, "You will be interested the day you die!" He said something that I couldn't figure out, so I said, "Why do you hate Jesus so much?" Now I will say that sometimes to certain people. It is a statement that I use rarely, but will use it when I think it is necessary. I am trying to get certain people to realize that they don't hate life, they don't hate their job, they don't hate me; they really

"Why do you hate Jesus so much?" Now I will say that sometimes to certain people. It is a statement that I use rarely, but will use it when I think it is necessary. I am trying to get certain people to realize that they don't hate life, they don't hate their job, they don't hate me; they really hate Jesus and that is the root cause of all of their problems.

hate Jesus and that is the root cause of all of their problems. I have had some very interesting conversations once I throw that question out there. He responded, "I don't hate Jesus, I hate you!" Now my usual response to this statement is, "You can't hate me, because you don't know me." That really gets people thinking. But before I could say anything, he backed his SUV up and began to leave.

So I walked over and began talking with one of the store clerks who was outside, and this guy came driving back over! He pulled up, rolled down his window and said to the clerk, "Why don't you get these religious people out of this gas station?" The only problem was that she was standing there reading one of the books that I had given her and had just told me how much she liked it! So I decided to walk towards his car. That may not have been a good move at that point, but I decided to anyway. The guy reached in between his seat and the console and pulled out a gun! Not what I was planning for my Sunday afternoon! But I had already thought about when this scenario was going to happen in my life. I knew it would occur at some point, I just didn't know when. The funny thing was, I wasn't half as nervous as I thought I would be. All of the sudden his hand shook. I don't know if he got nervous or an angel tapped his hand, but he dropped the gun back down in between the seat again. I walked towards the car, and very nicely, I said, "I share this with you, because I care about your soul, and I care where you are going to spend eternity." After I said that, he just stared at me, and I turned and walked away. Remember folks, watchmen don't have to worry about bullets. All a bullet can do is send us to be with the Person that we want to be with for all of eternity a little more quickly than we thought we would get there!

Philippians 1:21: "For to me to live is Christ, and to die is gain."

He had tried to commit suicide by driving his truck into a tree at 70 mph with no seat belt! But, the tree broke, his car flipped twice and landed in a church parking lot! He had some scratches on his face and a bruised chest and that was it. He got out of his car and walked away from that accident. He told me he asked, "God, why did you let me live?"

I used to wonder why my car keeps needing repairs, but I have finally figured out that it has nothing to do with my car, but with the souls I will meet at the auto shop! One of the last times I had to get my car fixed, Nate was running the shop. He was a 23-year-old former soldier. He had tried to commit suicide by driving his truck into a tree at 70 mph with no seat belt! But, the tree broke, his car flipped twice and landed in a church parking lot! He had some scratches on his face and a bruised chest and that was it. He got out of his car and walked away from that accident. He told me he asked, "God, why did you let me live?" I let him know the reason why God allowed him to live! I had prayed to go to the right place to get my car fixed and of course God answered that prayer!

I told the story about Nate at a conference in New Jersey one time, and a man came up to me afterward with tears in his eyes. He had recently decided to commit suicide, and was going to run his car into a tree to do it! He had already picked out the tree. After he heard the story, he knew he needed to repent of his sins and become born again. Praise the Lord!

1 Thessalonians 5:16-18: "Rejoice evermore. Pray without ceasing. In every thing give thanks: for this is the will of God in Christ Jesus concerning you."

One of my favorite ministers is Dr. Noah Hutchings of Southwest Radio Church Ministries (www. swrc.com), and he has a very simple saying that I love so much: "God is still on the throne. . . and prayer changes things."

God is still on His throne. He doesn't take days off. We might, but He doesn't.

Watchmen always know that God is still on His throne. He doesn't take days off. We might, but He doesn't. And watchmen always know prayer changes things. There might be some long nights standing on the wall before you have to blow the trumpet. So be ready to use that time wisely in prayer. God is in the business of listening to watchmen who obey Him!

Watchmen love to give and love
to look for opportunities
in which the Lord is opening
doors to do just that.

Chapter 6
More Blessed to Give Than Receive

"Do all the good you can, in all the ways you can, to all the souls
you can, in every place you can, at all the times you can, with
all the zeal you can, as long as ever you can."[10]
–JOHN WESLEY

Each of us needs encouragement as we live this life for God.

Deuteronomy 3:28: "But charge Joshua, and encourage him, and
strengthen him: for he shall go over before this people, and he shall
cause them to inherit the land which thou shalt see."

Here is the great leader Joshua, who we will later read
about in the book of Joshua, receiving a charge from the
people around him. They encouraged him to be the leader
that God had planned for him to be. Yes, even leaders need
encouragement!

1 Thessalonians 5:11: "Wherefore comfort yourselves together, and
edify one another, even as also ye do."

The word 'edify' here means to build up, or to erect something. It infers a growth in Christian wisdom. Are you doing
that in people's lives? Are you investing in people eternally, so
that they will not miss out on the plans God has for them?

Years ago, I used to teach at an all boys school in Baton
Rouge, Louisiana. When I left to move back to Atlanta, a lot
of the students wrote me letters. One of the letters I received
had an interesting sentence in it. It said, "Mr. Cahill, the only
reason I think God put you on planet earth was to encourage
other people." What a neat thing to hear from a young man.
We all need encouragement and that encouraged me!

It has been fun to watch what happens in the lives of some of the people in whom I have invested my time and materials. I have to be honest and say that some of those people have far surpassed me, and I am truly humbled by their boldness and love for others. I am totally fine with the fact that they have left me in their dust and are serving God passionately with their whole lives! What more could a teacher want than for his students to 'get it,' and to totally understand why they were placed on earth?

Nothing would make me happier than for you to read this book and then put it down and literally become the greatest watchman your family, friends, strangers, and your entire city has ever seen! And please don't forget that is what God wants to happen in your life as well.

> **Numbers 6:24-26:** "The LORD bless thee, and keep thee: The LORD make his face shine upon thee, and be gracious unto thee: The LORD lift up his countenance upon thee, and give thee peace."

Those words in Numbers 6 are one of the great Jewish blessings. Who wouldn't want that to happen in their lives? But let's turn it around. Are you being gracious to people? Does your character line up with your words? Are you being gracious as you are out there reaching the lost? Who we are and what we say will always go together!

> **Proverbs 15:13:** "A merry heart maketh a cheerful countenance: but by sorrow of the heart the spirit is broken."

One person I know prays that nothing on his countenance would push people away from him, but that his countenance would draw people to him for a conversation. Now that is a neat prayer. He knows that God can use everything about him to glorify His name.

> **Psalm 145:8:** "The LORD *is* gracious, and full of compassion; slow to anger, and of great mercy."

In Psalm 136, it says 26 times: "for his mercy endureth forever." And you know what? So should ours! Be merciful to others as you are sharing your faith.

Proverbs 15:1: "A soft answer turneth away wrath: but grievous words stir up anger."

Answer with a soft word when someone gets angry. If someone raises their voice in a conversation, lower yours. It will usually lead to a much longer chat.

... "Will you pray for me?" If you ever get that answer...say, "Let's pray."

One thing I ask people a lot at the end of a conversation is, "Is there anything that I can do for you?" Many times one of the things they will say is, "Will you pray for me?" If you ever get that answer, don't say yes. Go ahead and say, "Let's pray." Bow your head and start praying! Many people have never heard their name taken to the throne of God before. Sometimes I will put my hand on their shoulder as I pray. I have seen people's entire countenance change when I pray for them like that. Remember that a smile, a pat on the shoulder, or the simple shaking of a hand can go a long way in people's lives.

One time when I was speaking in Los Angeles, I got sick. God was gracious to me and got me through all of my speaking, but when I got to LAX to return home, I was dreading the four and a half hour plane flight. I didn't want to talk with anyone; I just wanted to sit down and relax. So when I sat down, I looked at the man next to me and basically said, "Hi. My name is Mark Cahill. I believe in Jesus and here is one of the books that I wrote. Have a nice flight!" Okay, that wasn't exactly what I said, but that is what I meant with whatever I did say! He said, "That is interesting." Oh no–I didn't want that to be interesting, I wanted to be left alone! I said, "Why is that interesting?" Well you have probably guessed correctly: I didn't get much rest on that flight! He was the director of a TV series called *The Vampire Diaries*. He was flying to Atlanta to film one of the episodes. As we kept talking, he let me know that he started as a cameraman and had worked his way up to becoming a director. He was a very interesting man. But then he told me that one of the other cameramen that he worked with became a Christian and began to witness to him. He listened intently but had not made a commitment to Jesus. He then said that the cameraman told him that there were certain things that he could not film anymore because they went against his beliefs.

Psalm 101:3: "I will set no wicked thing before mine eyes: I hate the work of them that turn aside; *it* shall not cleave to me."

That cameraman was a man of conviction. He didn't want to set any worthless thing in front of his eyes. That really spoke volumes to the director. That man finally left the film industry and is now a missionary in Kenya. But don't forget that he was also a missionary in Hollywood before he was ever a missionary in Kenya!

1 Corinthians 3:6: "I have planted, Apollos watered; but God gave the increase."

It was nice to come along and water the seed that the cameraman had planted in that director's life. It made it so much easier to talk with him, because he had already met a watchman with conviction.

1 Corinthians 10:31: "Whether therefore ye eat, or drink, or whatsoever ye do, do all to the glory of God."

It was during the time that I was teaching at the all boys school in Baton Rouge that evangelist Jimmy Swaggart fell into

his sin. There was a lot of whooping and hollering at the school when he fell. One of the teachers, Mr. Davis, asked me what I thought about it. I said, "It is not a good day when a man of God falls into sin." He looked at me and said, "You really are a Christian, aren't you?" You don't know when people are going to have their eyes upon you. It might be just to see your reaction to something like that. That is why we always have to be humble and gracious when we are out and about with others.

...when it comes to people in cults, they have been deceived, and you shouldn't get mad at them. We should be more upset with the Great Deceiver than we are with them.

Remember that when it comes to people in cults, they have been deceived, and you shouldn't get mad at them. We should be more upset with the Great Deceiver than we are with them. As a friend told me once, if a blind man falls down in front of you, would you laugh at him? Of course not. You would help him up. The same principle is true here. When people fall into false teachings, remember that they are blind. We should help them up and lead them in the right way.

> **Luke 6:38:** "Give, and it shall be given unto you; good measure, pressed down, and shaken together, and running over, shall men give into your bosom. For with the same measure that ye mete withal it shall be measured to you again."

I want to challenge you as a watchman to be a giver. And I do mean a giver. Not being stingy. Not giving to see what you can get back. But being a Christ-like giver.

> **Acts 20:35:** "I have shewed you all things, how that so labouring ye ought to support the weak, and to remember the words of the Lord

Jesus, how he said, It is more blessed to give than to receive."

When He says it is more blessed to give than receive, He means it. Why? There is so much more going on when you give to someone than you can ever realize.

Jesus doesn't mince his words anywhere in the Bible. He means business. When He says it is more blessed to give than receive, He means it. Why? There is so much more going on when you give to someone than you can ever realize. This world comes down to selfishness and selflessness. It is really one or the other with people. You see people with the attitude of, 'don't touch my stuff,' all the way to others trying to see who they can bless each day. And as a watchman, there is only one of those two categories you are allowed to fall into!

At a gas station one day, I walked over and inserted my card into the gas pump to pay for a lady's gas. I let her know that Jesus said it is more blessed to give than receive, and that I try to live by those words. The lady told me that she had just come from a church service where the preacher talked about giving, and now she got to 'see it lived out!' When I got my credit card bill, I had paid for a $74 tank of gas! I think I will pick a motorcycle next time (Just kidding!)!

Once at a store, I gave some books out to folks who were shopping, and then as I was standing in line, I paid for the items of the woman behind me, and also told her what Jesus had said. She was very appreciative. So I went to my car to get a couple more books for people inside, and as I walked back in, I looked over and saw the lady sitting in her car crying. So I walked over to see if she was okay, and she let me know that she was going through some tough times and was very grateful. I said, "Are you born again?" She said, "No, I am Catholic." So we had a great talk about what being born again means, and I was able to bless her some more.

At the train station at one airport, I bought about ten tokens and then waited for the people that were coming in from other cities, and handed them a free token along with a gospel tract. I would tell them what Jesus said. One lady looked at me and said, "I sure wish there were more Christians like you." Remember folks that people know Christians are supposed to be givers.

> **John 3:16:** "For God so loved the world, that he gave his only begotten Son, that whosoever believeth in him should not perish, but have everlasting life."

Since God was a giver, those who follow Him are supposed to be givers as well.

When I ride my bike for some exercise, I always bring a plastic bag with $10 bills and gospel tracts in it. One of my goals on those days is to make sure that I come home with no money! It is fun to stop at bus stops and bless people, and stop along the way and have conversations with people. Those conversations are also a good time for me to rest on those hot Atlanta days, too!

Whenever I go through a tollbooth, I witness to the attendant, and then pay for the toll of the car behind me. I also give the attendant one of my books and ask them to give it to the driver and let them know a Christian man paid for their toll that day, because Jesus said it was more blessed to give than receive. Travelling through a tollbooth in Oklahoma one day, I paid and then drove away slowly and watched through my rearview mirror to see what would happen. The person tried to hand money through the window and the tollbooth operator wouldn't take it and handed the book to them! I love it when lost people hand out Christian material. And sadly, some of those lost people are being better watchmen than some people who are reading this book right now. So as I drove away, all the cars blended in together, but wouldn't you know that a little bit later down the highway, this car passes me, I look over, and the passenger is intently reading the book that I had given to the tollbooth worker! Praise the Lord!

I had the opportunity to sit next to an atheist one day on a plane flight. He just railed against God and against Christians. He called this one church in Atlanta, "Fort God" because it was a multimillion-dollar structure. He said Christians just take and take and take. So when I finished our conversation, I gave him one of my books. He told me that he thought it was very gracious of me to give him a book and loved that my website is by donation only. Then David told me about his secretary that was this wonderful Christian lady. He really liked her so much. You see, he wasn't being truthful. All Christians aren't takers. He watches this lady all the time and sees a beautiful Christian woman, and he knows it. Never forget that how we live our lives matter!

> **Malachi 3:8-10:** "Will a man rob God? Yet ye have robbed me. But ye say, Wherein have we robbed thee? In tithes and offerings. Ye *are* cursed with a curse: for ye have robbed me, *even* this whole nation. Bring ye all the tithes into the storehouse, that there may be meat in mine house, and prove me now herewith, saith the LORD of hosts, if I will not open you the windows of heaven, and pour you out a blessing, that *there shall* not *be room* enough *to receive it.*"

Now we all know stealing is wrong, but can you imagine if you actually stole from God? Just think about that for a second. But do you know if you don't tithe to God, you are stealing from Him? Now none of us would steal from the government, because we know there is a consequence to that. But many of us will steal from God and think nothing of it. Trust me, there will be a consequence for that, too. But watchmen don't act like that. They are looking for reasons to give and to bless others. Plus, you may want to read the previous verse again, because God is talking not just about tithes, but offerings as well–above and beyond the requirement. I never look at my tithe as the highest I will give, but the lowest I will give. I want to be in offering mode, or giving mode, and stay there all the days of my life.

You see, giving is a heart issue. It really has nothing to do with how much money you do or don't have. Your heart is what wants to give when you follow the Lord.

2 Corinthians 9:6, 7: "But this *I say*, He which soweth sparingly shall reap also sparingly; and he which soweth bountifully shall reap also bountifully. Every man according as he purposeth in his heart, *so let him give*; not grudgingly, or of necessity: for God loveth a cheerful giver."

You see, giving is a heart issue. It really has nothing to do with how much money you do or don't have. Your heart is what wants to give when you follow the Lord. You are cheerful when you can bless someone else. You are looking for ways to bless someone. Your eyes are open for opportunities to reach out and touch someone's life.

I was reading an article once about Kurt Warner, the famous pro football player. In the article, it said that when he and his family go out to eat, that they will always pick up the meal of someone else in the restaurant. The article then stated that his kids would look around the restaurant and say, "Hey dad, what about that table? Or, what about that one?" I just couldn't believe this as I was reading it. He was teaching his kids that as Christians, we are givers, and you find ways to bless others. And he was modeling that to his children! My kind of dad! As I was reading the article, I decided that if Kurt Warner can do that, so can I! So almost every time I am at a restaurant, I pick up someone else's meal. Boy, does it get interesting sometimes!

Sitting in a restaurant one day with the point guard from my college team and his family, I looked over and saw these two 50-year-old men eating. They just looked like two good buddies having a good time. So I told my waitress that I would like to pay for their meal. She was surprised by that. I have actually had some waitresses tell me that was the coolest thing they have ever seen in their restaurant! You see, when we bless others, God is working in ways that we don't even realize.

So when the waitress told the men that someone had picked up their tab, they were shocked. So I walked over and struck up a conversation. I let them know what Jesus said. One guy looked at me dumbfounded. He said, "In all my years of being alive, I have never had anyone pick up a meal for me before." As we kept talking, the other guy had tears well up in his eyes as his mom had passed away recently. Neither man was born again, but we talked about what that means. They each took a book, shook my hand, and were on their way.

At one restaurant in Cincinnati, I stopped and talked to a man who was holding his daughter and staring up at a football game on television. As we were chatting, he told me that his daughter wasn't healthy and had already had a bunch of surgeries. It was pretty sad, but it was great to see the love of a father for his daughter! So I asked my waitress to give me that table's bill. It was a table of five or six. After they ate, they stopped by our table and thanked us for being such a blessing to them. The grandmother emailed me a couple of weeks later and told me that she had told so many people about that encounter. Nothing like that had ever happened to her before. She had a pretty strong faith in Jesus Christ, and it really encouraged her to live out her faith more!

> **Luke 18:12-14:** "I fast twice in the week, I give tithes of all that I possess. And the publican, standing afar off, would not lift up so much as *his* eyes unto heaven, but smote upon his breast, saying, God be merciful to me a sinner. I tell you, this man went down to his house

justified *rather* than the other: for every one that exalteth himself shall be abased; and he that humbleth himself shall be exalted."

We really have to watch our attitude when we give. I don't tell you these stories to say, 'Hey look at me.' I share with you, so you see

We really have to watch our attitude when we give.

what God can do when you become a giver. He can literally work wonders right before your eyes. I want you to see those wonders before you take your last breath and see even more how wonderful He is!

One summer day when I was still a teacher, I was driving into school and saw some prisoners outside whacking weeds, so I went to the convenience store and bought Gatorades for them and the guards. I went and gave them all Gatorades, had a short talk with some of them and gave them some tracts. Later that day as I was leaving school, the men were still out there. They had a long, hot day in the Georgia sun. They remembered my car, and one by one, they stepped up to the roadway with big smiles and a wave of the hand thanking me for blessing them that day. It brings me to tears writing that. Just the simple gesture of recognizing someone as a special creation of the Most High God can go a long, long way in that person's life. Please remember people are fearfully and wonderfully made in the eyes of God, and we need to treat them that way as well.

Psalm 139:14: "I will praise thee; for I am fearfully *and* wonderfully made: marvellous *are* thy works; and *that* my soul knoweth right well."

Never forget that we as Christians are the ones who are supposed to be setting the standards for those around us. Let's set that standard very high. Serving God is challenging, but watchmen are up to the challenge!

So let's say that you had zero money. Nothing. Could you still be a giver? Of course you can! When we give to the Lord, we can give time, tithes, and talent! There are many ways to bless other people, so just find out what those ways are.

One lady she told me that she had a garage sale just so she could witness to others that came by! Another person told me that they had a garage sale where everything was free! They even advertised it in the paper that way. Let's just say they had a ton of people show up and then they freely gave the gospel away as well!

Some friends of mine always seem to be having someone over for dinner or someone staying in an extra room at their house. They bless others with their talents of preparing a wonderful meal, and then talk about the Lord over that meal.

Once when I was talking with a worship leader at an event where I was speaking, he told me that when he was young, he hitchhiked to Panama City to party. The first guy that picked him up was the pastor of a church, and the pastor shared the gospel with him. The second guy that picked him up was a pastor of a church, and he also shared the gospel with him. When the third guy picked him up, he said to the driver, "I know. You are a pastor of a church!" The pastor said, "How did you know that?" By the time he got to Panama City, six people had given him a ride and all six were pastors of churches! So we can bless people with a ride and have it lead to a gospel presentation, and any Christian can do that.

As one person said, "Little is much when God is in it!" Don't look at the amount or how big something is. Just be faithful. Watchmen are always faithful people.

Now I want you to be very careful about something. There is a movement going around called 'servant evangelism.' It is where people go out and do nice things for people, such as mowing everyone in the neighborhood's grass, cleaning up trash along the streets, wrapping Christmas presents for free at the mall, etc. And people are calling this evangelism. But, it is not.

I was speaking at a camp in Tennessee one summer, and we took the teens to the streets of Chattanooga to witness. One of the leaders also provided the opportunity for the students to walk the streets of Chattanooga and pick up trash. He told them this was 'servant evangelism.' Well we did have a lot of kids sign up for that group! And that

...people go out and do nice things for people, such as mowing everyone in the neighborhood's grass...
And people are calling this evangelism. But, it is not.

group did absolutely nothing to get anybody ready for eternity. It might make your flesh feel good to do something nice, but it does nothing to impact someone's eternal destination. If I saw a bunch of people cleaning up the streets, my first thought would be that they were prisoners! They got in trouble with the law and are having to do community service because of that. It would never cross my mind that these folks are Christians, so let me go to the store, buy a Bible, and see if Jesus was really who He said He was. Never in a million years would I think that was a group of Christians.

On the same trip, I was walking the streets and ran into some of our students witnessing to a guy out on a sidewalk. The reason they were there was because they had been kicked out of a restaurant for witnessing, and the bartender wanted to talk some more, so he walked outside to continue the conversation about our Lord! Now those students were being watchmen!

I have met two different people who went evangelizing in Boston with two different groups. They both told me they did the same thing. They would go to the train stations and hand

Does performing good works replace verbally sharing the gospel? Absolutely not!!!

out free granola bars to people. Yes, that is it. Nothing else. Just free granola bars. One of the men told me that some of the riders of the trains knew that they were Christians, so they wouldn't take the granola bars! So wouldn't it be better to try and hand them a gospel tract and have them say 'no' to that rather than trying to hand them a granola bar that they refuse? Of course it would be. Wouldn't it be better to open up your mouth and let people know Jesus died for their sins or that Judgment Day is coming when they are not even going to take your granola bars anyway? Of course it would be.

One of those men told me that they do that because people in the Northeast are so hard-hearted toward the gospel that this will soften their hearts. Well that is interesting. I know of a group of people that witness every Saturday at an abortion clinic by the Yale University campus in Connecticut and talk with ladies getting abortions, students, and professors all the time. No granola bars necessary!

Does performing good works replace verbally sharing the gospel? Absolutely not!!!

> **Mark 16:15:** "And he said unto them, Go ye into all the world, and preach the gospel to every creature."

The word 'preach' here is not the word 'preacher.' All the word 'preach' means is to proclaim openly. It means to speak of something that has gravity or authority to it. It is so important that it should be obeyed. Folks, that is the gospel. It is so important it must be proclaimed. And for the lost person, it is so important, they must believe.

One pastor told me that he calls doing nice things for people 'pre-evangelism,' but it is not evangelism. A watchmen always knows to do what the Bible says and not to do what might just feel good to your flesh, but isn't biblical.

Remember that the gospel is a verbal proclamation and not a visual demonstration.

Leaving Toronto one day, I struck up a conversation with the shoeshine man! He was sitting there doing nothing. One thing I look for is people killing time. Someone sitting on a park bench, meandering through a mall, bored at his or her job, etc. Why not help them kill their time in a positive way! He had grown up Catholic and was now a Muslim. So trust me, we were having an interesting conversation. Well all of the sudden a guy comes up to get his shoes shined! So he sits down and the man keeps talking to me. As you have probably figured out, the guy getting his shoes shined now gets the opportunity to listen in! I call this indirect witnessing. You are talking to one person, but others are listening in to the conversation. And sometimes they are the ones you might really be there for. I ended up paying for the guy's shoes that were shined, left a good tip for the shoe shiner, and then walked away in a conversation with the man with newly shined shoes!

One time, God granted me an amazing opportunity to witness to Tiger Woods when I was in Orlando. I was heading home after it happened, and I told the story to the man next to me on the flight. When we stood up to leave, the guy behind me tapped me on the shoulder and said, "You got the chance to witness to Tiger?" I told him that I had, and he said he would like to talk with me after we got off the plane. As we stood outside and chatted for a bit, he told me that he was one of a group of 30 men that were praying for the salvation of Tiger's soul! Wow! So I let him know that I was part of the answer to their prayers! God literally opened up the door out of nowhere. Sometimes you don't know who is listening when you are speaking, but watchmen always know it is their job to speak!

Often people tell me that they would die for Jesus, but how is that possible if we won't even give what's in our pockets for Jesus?

Jacob said to Esau in Genesis 33:11, "Take, I pray thee, my blessing that is brought to thee; because God hath dealt graciously with me, and because I have enough. And he urged him, and he took *it*."

Remember watchmen, as the days run short, tough times are ahead in this world. But Christians are not hoarders, we are givers! We look for opportunities to bless others. It is in our DNA once we are believers. We can't wait for the opportunity for God's love to overflow through us into others' lives.

I was standing over a credit card receipt one day at a restaurant figuring out what to leave Natasha as a tip. My plan was to give her a $100 tip, as her young son was having a lot of medical issues. But as I stood there, everything in me said to make it $200! That is a lot of money where I come from. We are not called to hoard, though. And when the Lord is leading, we are commanded to follow. So that is the tip that I left her. When I gave her the receipt, she just began to weep. I found out the next day from a friend of hers that one week earlier, Natasha's purse had been stolen, and you guessed it: She had $200 in her purse! She has emailed me letting me know that she knew for sure that it was God who led me there that day, and that she is searching now to find out what real Biblical salvation is.

John 15:13: "Greater love hath no man than this, that a man lay down his life for his friends."

Jesus knew the importance of laying down His life for the sins of all of mankind. Often people tell me that they would die for Jesus, but how is that possible if we won't even give what's in our pockets for Jesus? We won't even give our time and talents to the Lord, and yet we think we will die for Jesus one day if it came to that. I'm sorry, it doesn't work that way.

1 Timothy 6:7: "For we brought nothing into *this* world, and *it is* certain we can carry nothing out."

You are not taking anything with you when you die, so you might as well send it on ahead! It is time to lay it all down for the Lord.

1 Corinthians 3:11-15: "For other foundation can no man lay than that is laid, which is Jesus Christ. Now if any man build upon this foundation gold, silver, precious stones, wood, hay, stubble; Every man's work shall be made manifest: for the day shall declare it, because it shall be revealed by fire; and the fire shall try every man's work of what sort it is. If any man's work abide which he hath built thereupon, he shall receive a reward. If any man's work shall be burned, he shall suffer loss: but he himself shall be saved; yet so as by fire."

There is a reward day in heaven for believers. Your works will be judged. That is not the day you want to be a pauper. God wants to shower you with rewards for the life that you lived on earth for Him. All I know is that if the same God Who has given us His Son has something else to give us, we want it! It literally has to be beyond wonderful!

Matthew 7:12: "Therefore all things whatsoever ye would that men should do to you, do ye even so to them: for this is the law and the prophets."

This is what people call the Golden Rule. Remember that all of us can be down and out in life at some point. I have had zero dollars a couple of times in my life. But God was more than faithful to bring people along to help me out. It made my faith in Him grow by leaps and bounds!

Acts 10:1-4: "There was a certain man in Caesarea called Cornelius, a centurion of the band called the Italian *band*, A devout *man*, and one that feared God with all his house, which gave much alms to the people, and prayed to God alway. He saw in a vision evidently about the ninth hour of the day an angel of God coming in to him, and saying unto him, Cornelius. And when he looked on him, he was afraid, and said, What is it, Lord? And he said unto him, Thy prayers and thine alms are come up for a memorial before God."

So if your alms or your giving came up before the Lord, how would it look? Stop for a second and think about that. If you don't like the answer, do something about it.

Do you need to stop buying dessert, so that you can leave a better tip? Do you need to get rid of your cell phone to have more money to give away? I am amazed at how many people tell me that a cell phone is a necessity, but giving to the Lord's work is an afterthought. Do you need to get rid of cable television and take that extra money and give it to a missionary? All that box is doing is polluting your mind and stealing your time. Think about it. Do you need to stop going to movies, take that money and buy some tracts, and go back to the same movie theater and do some witnessing for the Lord?

Galatians 6:7-10: "Be not deceived; God is not mocked: for whatsoever a man soweth, that shall he also reap. For he that soweth to his flesh shall of the flesh reap corruption; but he that soweth to the Spirit shall of the Spirit reap life everlasting. And let us not be weary in well doing: for in due season we shall reap, if we faint not. As we have therefore opportunity, let us do good unto all *men*, especially unto them who are of the household of faith."

Travelling home from the airport one day, I was sitting on the train and struck up a conversation with an older black woman. The contrast of her graying hair and the color of her face was a beautiful sight. She had a warm smile and was just a lovely lady. More importantly, she had a great relationship with Jesus Christ. She told me that a week earlier, her purse had been stolen. It had all of her money in it. She explained she didn't need a bank to keep her money in; all she needed was a purse. So I opened my bag and took out an envelope filled with the money that I had received for books from my speaking event. I took the checks out that were addressed to me, and folded the top of the envelope down. I still to this day have no clue how much money was in there. I reached across the aisle and handed the lady the envelope. She opened the envelope and if you could have seen the look on her face! Priceless!! She just sat there and cried. I don't know how much money was in there, but to her, it was a million dollars! I am so glad when God gives me an opportunity to bless those who are of the household of faith!

> **1 Corinthians 13:13:** "And now abideth faith, hope, charity, these three; but the greatest of these *is* charity."

The word 'charity' here means brotherly love, good will, and benevolence. As I always tell people, ***the lost may argue with the truths we share, but they can never argue with the love we show***. There should be no one–and I do mean no one– that can out love you in your family, neighborhood, or workplace all the days of your life. Be a great giver, a great source of Biblical truth, and a great lover all of your days.

Remember, watchmen are always gracious to people. You can speak strongly and still be gracious. Watchmen love to encourage both the lost and the saved. Watchmen love to give and love to look for opportunities in which the Lord is opening doors to do just that. Watchmen always know it is more blessed to give than receive. Watchmen don't grow weary in doing good. You will reap a harvest if you do not faint before the finish line of life!

Watchmen always know it is more blessed to give than to receive.

Are you turning your family, your neighborhood, your school, your workplace, and your city upside down for Jesus Christ?

Chapter 7
"I Think About Eternity All the Time."

"At the timberline where the storms strike with the most fury,
the sturdiest trees are found."[11]
–HUDSON TAYLOR

O ne of my favorite chapters in the entire Bible is Acts 17, and you are about to find out why! Make sure you are ready, because it is loaded with information that every watchman needs to know!

> **Acts 17:1, 2:** "Now when they had passed through Amphipolis and Apollonia, they came to Thessalonica, where was a synagogue of the Jews: And Paul, as his manner was, went in unto them, and three sabbath days reasoned with them out of the scriptures,"

A very interesting term that is used here is 'as his manner was.' You see, it was a natural part of Paul's life to talk to the lost. He did it everywhere he went. It wasn't an odd thing. That is how it should be for you and me. Everywhere we go–even if we're just running errands–should be seen as an opportunity to plant a seed for our Lord.

Once when I was speaking in Cincinnati, I had a good chat with the cleaning lady at my hotel. She told me that she'd been working there for five years. I asked her, "In those five years, how many Christians have taken the time to share with you what I just shared with you?" She said, "Two." I was the second person. So do you think only two Christians have ever stayed at that hotel? How many more post office workers, waitresses, UPS guys, flight attendants, and cashiers are we going to walk past and not warn about the upcoming Judgment? Let that never be named amongst you!

It is very important to use the Word of God when you are witnessing. Why? You want to make sure that if the person wants to argue, they will have to argue against God's words.

Acts 17 also says that Paul 'reasoned with them.' Questions and answers. Conversations go back and forth, and we want to get people thinking. People have to be thinking about eternity and God before they can get saved. So we want to get the wheels in their heads spinning on the topic.

Isaiah 1:18: "Come now, and let us reason together, saith the LORD: though your sins be as scarlet, they shall be as white as snow; though they be red like crimson, they shall be as wool."

How did Paul reason with them? Out of the Scriptures. It is very important to use the Word of God when you are witnessing. Why? You want to make sure that if the person wants to argue, they will have to argue against God's words. Remember that the Bible has stood the test of time. So even if you never see that person again, your words can encourage them to go to the Bible to find the truths of God.

Acts 17:3: "Opening and alleging, that Christ must needs have suffered, and risen again from the dead; and that this Jesus, whom I preach unto you, is Christ."

Paul always preached Christ crucified. Why? Because that is the only way people's sins were going to be forgiven.

1 Corinthians 1:23: "But we preach Christ crucified, unto the Jews a stumblingblock, and unto the Greeks foolishness;"

Remember when Jesus said to Peter in Matthew 16:15, "He saith unto them, But whom say ye that I am?"

That is a personal question. He doesn't want to know what everyone's opinion of Him is. He wanted to know what Peter thought! So ask people in your conversations: Who do you think Jesus is? It is a great question.

> **Acts 17:4:** "And some of them believed, and consorted with Paul and Silas; and of the devout Greeks a great multitude, and of the chief women not a few."

God allowed Paul to see some of the fruit of his ministry. Would you press on even if you didn't see any of the fruit of what you are doing for the Lord?

I was witnessing in a mall one day, and it was not going well! Two and a half hours in the mall, and I didn't feel like I had done much of anything. Plus, the last guy I had chatted with was pretty mean and rejected me big time! So at that point, I said to myself, 'That's it! I am out of here!' But as I started walking out of the mall, I saw a lady walking down a hallway, and I decided to stop her and try one more conversation before I left. Just a few minutes into the conversation, the lady really began to open up, and I could feel the Lord lay down deep within my heart that this lady was the whole reason I went to the mall that day! I am so glad that I didn't throw in the towel earlier in the day when I didn't think things were going my way. We ended up having a wonderful thirty-minute talk on the truths of God!

> **Acts 17: 5, 6:** "But the Jews which believed not, moved with envy, took unto them certain lewd fellows of the baser sort, and gathered a company, and set all the city on an uproar, and assaulted the house of Jason, and sought to bring them out to the people. And when they found them not, they drew Jason and certain brethren unto the rulers of the city, crying, These that have turned the world upside down are come hither also;"

So let's ask a simple question: Are you turning your family, your neighborhood, your school, your workplace, and your city upside down for Jesus Christ? Remember when you read the Scriptures, it is Christians that cause trouble in cities. But

Always have a readiness of mind when you open up the Scriptures. Ask God to give you a nugget of truth every time that you read His word, and He will!

they do it very differently than lost people do. They do it through love, they do it through preaching the word, and they do it through living a holy life. And when others in the city follow suit, it changes the whole town!!

Also don't forget that all of us have reputations. What is yours? Do people look at you and say, 'That is a follower of Jesus, no doubt about it'? If not, then today is the day to get back on track.

Acts 17:7: "Whom Jason hath received: and these all do contrary to the decrees of Caesar, saying that there is another king, *one* Jesus."

Keep telling people who the real Jesus is! I was talking to a French Canadian from Quebec one day in the airport. We were chatting about different things, and we were fine, until I asked him: "Who do you think Jesus is?" Then suddenly he said, "Oh, my English isn't that good," and he started talking to his buddies in French! Well his English was just fine until I asked that question! That is why it is a good question. So then I started talking to his buddies, and one of them even took one of my books!

Acts 17:8-11: "And they troubled the people and the rulers of the city, when they heard these things. And when they had taken security of Jason, and of the other, they let them go. And the brethren immediately sent away Paul and Silas by night unto Berea: who coming *thither* went into the synagogue of the Jews. These were more noble than those in Thessalonica, in that they received the word with all readiness of mind, and searched the scriptures daily, whether those things were so."

Always have a readiness of mind when you open up the Scriptures. Ask God to give you a nugget of truth every time that you read His word, and He will! Reading and studying the Word of God is a daily part of our walk with God.

These Bereans had to encourage Paul's heart. He found a group of people who were going to test what he said against the proven truths of God's Word. Watchmen need to be like the Bereans and test everything against the Scriptures. Since these people were doing just that, Paul knew that they were going to do great things for God!

Challenge lost people to read the Bible. Many lost people have opinions about God's Word. I will ask them, "Do you ever read the Bible?" And so many times the answer is no. If they have an opinion about a document they don't read, we should encourage them to read it!

An easy way to do that with a friend is to read the Gospel of John together. Read one chapter a day, and call each other at 9 o'clock at night and discuss it. It will only take you 21 days to go through the book, and only great things are going to come from both of you reading the Bible!

> **Romans 10:17:** "So then faith *cometh* by hearing, and hearing by the word of God."

> **Acts 17:12-16:** "Therefore many of them believed; also of honourable women which were Greeks, and of men, not a few. But when the Jews of Thessalonica had knowledge that the word of God was preached of Paul at Berea, they came thither also, and stirred up the people. And then immediately the brethren sent away Paul to go as it were to the sea: but Silas and Timotheus abode there still. And they that conducted Paul brought him unto Athens: and receiving a commandment unto Silas and Timotheus for to come to him with all speed, they departed. Now while Paul waited for them at Athens, his spirit was stirred in him, when he saw the city wholly given to idolatry."

Sometimes waiting can be one of the great things we do in life. When we stop and wait, often we begin to think, and it is when we are stopping and thinking that God can really work in us. It is hard for that process to happen through all of the distractions of life.

Once when I took my Dad to the eye doctor, I struck up a conversation with a woman in the waiting room. She had grown up Mormon, but now didn't have much to do with religion. As our conversation got deeper, she began to cry. She knew she and her family needed to get serious about the things of God. I am glad I was there waiting with a purpose.

By the way, does it stir within your spirit when you see all of the idolatry in our world? The phrase in that passage means 'to arouse to anger.' Do you get angry at all the sin that is in the beautiful world God created? I'm sure you can easily list a billion things that people idolize in this world that have nothing to do with God. When is it going to stir inside your spirit to start doing something about it?

Each New Year's Eve, Atlanta has a Peach Drop, just like the ball drop in NYC. So that is one of the places I always go witnessing that night. All of these people come out to party, they count down the last ten seconds of the year, the peach drops, they make a lot of noise, and within twenty minutes, everybody is gone! It is the strangest thing.

Well one of my goals on that evening is to be talking to a lost person at the stroke of midnight. Why? I can't think of a better way to end the previous year or a better way to start the next one than talking to a lost person about Jesus Christ! This past year, I was talking with a Muslim named Ali when the countdown began. We were having a great talk. On the inside, I let out a big "Yes" as I accomplished one of my goals for the evening! He wished me a happy new year and then said, "Today is my birthday!" His birthday was January 1st! Well I wanted to make sure he never forgot that birthday, so I gave him one of my books and a financial blessing that was a gift from the Biblical Jesus. He was all smiles!

Paul's spirit stirred within him, because he was a man of conviction. Make sure you have that same type of biblical conviction, as well.

Acts 17:17: "Therefore disputed he in the synagogue with the Jews, and with the devout persons, and in the market daily with them that met with him."

Did Paul go sightseeing when he went to Athens? No. He confronted the lost with truth, and we need to do the same.

Never forget that we have a daily faith. It is not a weekly faith, a monthly faith, or a once a year mission trip faith.

Never forget that we have a daily faith. It is not a weekly faith, a monthly faith, or a once a year mission trip faith. We daily reach out to the lost every chance we get. When you walk out the door, you are on a mission trip. Period. It is really that simple.

So where are some places that we can go to get into these conversations?

College campuses are great places to go. That is where people swap ideas like you see here in Athens. People have all kinds of ideas, and they like to talk about them in this setting. Also remember this is where we are seeing so many Christians lose their faith. Now many of them truly lost their faith in middle school and high school, but they finally walk away from it in college. That's another reason why it's a great place to talk with people.

When I was in Cincinnati to speak recently, I decided to go over to the University of Cincinnati to do some witnessing. Nathan and I had a great conversation. He had on a pro-life shirt, so it was easy to get into our conversation. As we talked about murdering babies, the lady at the next table kept

You can save all the babies in the world, but if you are banking on your good deeds when you stand in front of a holy and pure God, you are in bad shape eternally.

looking at us! She probably looked over and listened three or four times throughout the conversation. Nathan, who was Roman Catholic, told me that it would be his good works that would get him to heaven. Do you see the red flag? That is biblically incorrect. You can save all the babies in the world, but if you are banking on your good deeds when you stand in front of a holy and pure God, you are in bad shape eternally. Nathan has already finished one of my books, and has emailed me a couple of times with questions and asking for some books for his friends! He is doing some thinking.

After talking to Nathan, I got into a conversation with Paul, a freshman, who was a real music lover and sang in a band. During our conversation, he told me, "I think about eternity all the time!" You never know whom you are going to meet. It might be someone who is struggling with what happens when we die. We talked for thirty minutes, and I gave him some materials to read. He stood up, shook my hand, and said, "Thanks for stopping by and talking!" Not everyone rejects you out there. Many people are very kind, gracious, and thankful. Paul was definitely one of those people.

After chatting with Paul, I ran into Akmal who was a student at the college, but was also working the front desk of my hotel when I checked in! We had an amazing talk about the Lord at the hotel and continued it at his college. He had grown up Muslim, and his uncle was an Imam! He wasn't much into it, and he wasn't into Christianity either, but he would definitely talk about it! Our job is to plant seeds. Keep planting them!

One of the topics you will almost certainly find brought into your conversations on a college campus (or high school and junior high for that matter) is evolution. Did we evolve from ape into man?

As Carl Kerby from Reasons for Hope states, "'Did God really say that?' is a great question. It's not deep, it's not theological; it's really very simple. God said one thing; the serpent said another. Adam and Eve blew it, because they decided they could use their wisdom to determine who was telling the truth. The problem is that we're doing the same thing today: We use our wisdom to determine truth, instead of God's Word."[12]

That is a key statement Carl is making. All evolution is really about is questioning the Word of God. There is no way to fit macro evolution into the Bible. People will try to do it, but they can't do it with what is written on the pages of God's Word.

"Do you know how many stars are in the sky? It's a huge number. To make it simple, when you look into the night sky, the one formation that stands out is the 'big dipper'. Inside the cup of the big dipper alone, just the cup, there are one billion stars. Not impressed? You shouldn't be, because it's not a billion 'stars', it's a billion GALAXIES in the cup of the big dipper. By the way, a galaxy holds a minimum of a million stars. It can be as high as a trillion stars. Our galaxy alone is estimated to be 200 billion stars. We don't know how to make a single star. How in the world could hydrogen gas pull itself together to form a single star, much less 70 sextillion (that's a seven followed by 22 zeros) observable stars. Also, the total number of stars, including the ones that we cannot see, is said by some to be infinite."[13]

By the way, how did this universe come together?

Genesis 1:1: "In the beginning God created the heaven and the earth."

Also in order for evolution to be true, a male human would have had to evolve in the exact same place at the exact same

Questions to ask people when you are having conversations about evolution:
- *How did life come from non-life?*
- *How did order come from disorder?*
- *If there was a big bang, where did the material come from that got banged?*

time as a female human, with both of their reproductive systems working perfectly in order for the human race to continue. It doesn't do any good for the male to evolve first and the female to evolve 100 years later. Or, for the male to evolve in America and the female to evolve in Europe with no way for them to get together. And not only that, you need to realize that would have to happen for every species on planet earth. I just saw an article that said there are more than eight million species! That means more than eight million times, a male of a species had to evolve at the exact same time and in the exact same place as the female of that species! Not only is the probability of that happening for even one species off the charts, how could it happen for eight million? It couldn't, and it didn't.

Here are some good questions to ask people when you are having conversations about evolution:
- How did life come from non-life?
- How did order come from disorder?
- If there was a big bang, where did the material come from that got banged?

For more information on the topic of creation vs. evolution go to:

www.creation.com
www.answersingenesis.org
www.rforh.com

Another great place to have conversations is a coffee shop. What do people sit around and do? They sit around and talk! And that is what you are looking for. So go in there and sit down next to someone and strike up a conversation.

Once in Fresno, CA, a bunch of us went out to witness, so we stopped at a coffee shop first and we all went and sat down at different people's tables! It was a lot of fun. I sat down at a table with two guys who were in their mid-twenties. As we started talking, one of them was a believer, and one wasn't. So I pretty much focused on the lost guy and helped him with some of his questions. I turned and looked a little bit later at the other guy. You could almost see this look of jealousy on his face. The look indicated that he knew he was supposed to be witnessing to his friend and not me! So when I finished, I stood up, shook some hands, and looked at the believer and said, "And now water that seed." It was a good encouragement for him to be bold for the Lord!

Malls are a wonderful place to go out and witness. I like to hit the malls during the Christmas season. Why? Sinners love buying gifts, and I like talking to them! So it is a perfect combination!

At a mall recently, I struck up a conversation with a security guard. He told me that he'd been in the military, and when he was in Afghanistan, he came back from a mission and realized that he was shot! He said the bullet went halfway through his bulletproof vest and part of the way into his chest. He said he had felt some warmth there, but the adrenalin must have just taken over to help him accomplish the mission. He told me that his mom was praying for him, because he wasn't saved, and being shot was a huge wake up call for him. She would talk to the lady who ran the church bookstore about him, and they would pray together for his salvation. So he came home from Afghanistan, started reading the Bible and going to church with his mom, and he decided to repent of his

I met a guy in the mall the other day who had become a Christian later in life. I said, "What happened along the way to lead you to make that decision?" He responded, "Sand in the shoe."

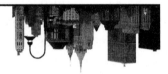

sins and get saved. Then he ended up getting married to the lady working in the church bookstore! Samuel had a great testimony to tell!!

Going through a mall once, I noticed a guy behind me walking with a cane. So I slowed down and said hello. I asked him if he was in the military, because he had a good military haircut! He said that he was. I asked him if he had been injured overseas, and he told me that he had been. I asked him if he felt comfortable telling me the story, and he began to tell me how he got both a brain and spine injury. He was with his squad on patrol, when an RPG hit their Humvee. His body was slammed so hard that he got a serious concussion that caused permanent brain and spine damage. He also had shrapnel in his arm, which was a combination of pieces of the RPG, and pieces of bone from one of the other soldiers who had the RPG go straight through both of his legs. Yet despite all of that, no one died during the incident.

So I asked him since he had been so close to death, what did he think happened when he died? That question led to a 45-minute walk through the mall as we discussed the topic! He told me that he was an ordained minister, did not really care what happened when you died as long as you followed Jesus down here, and that the Bible had been tampered with through the ages. I have come across people who have given me all of those responses before, so we had this amazing give and take. It was good challenging William with Biblical truth, and I just loved the conversation that we had.

I met a guy in the mall the other day who had become a Christian later in life. I said, "What happened along the way to lead you to make that decision?" He responded, "Sand in the shoe." I asked him what he meant by that. He told me that people got him thinking along the way of life and it just kept adding up and adding up and irritated him enough to search it out. You may have heard it said as a 'pebble in a shoe.' Remember, if you have ever had that happen, it gets irritating enough to stop, take your shoe off, and get that pebble out of there! The same principle applies here. We need to make sure we get people thinking. A good question, a good conversation, a good statement, or a good piece of literature can all get the wheels spinning in someone's head to lead them to search out what is true.

Another thing you can do is set up a Prayer Stop. (www.prayerstop.org) Setting up a Prayer Stop and offering people free prayer is a great idea! Very few people will turn down free prayer and that typically leads to some wonderful conversations.

How about witnessing to tailgaters at football games or handing tracts to people as they walk into the game? I just ran into two students that I taught 18 years ago when I was handing out tracts at a college football game! I had a lady at the same game tell me she already had the tract that I was handing out. I said, "Where did you get it?" She said, "The last game here!" We were there three months earlier, and she had gotten one of the tracts then!

Here is the story of Mitsuo Fuchida, the lead Japanese pilot who shouted the war cry, "Tora, Tora, Tora" on December 7, 1941 as he headed to Pearl Harbor:

> "I must admit, I was more excited than usual as I awoke that morning at 3:00 a.m., Hawaii time, four days past my thirty-ninth birthday. Our six aircraft carriers were positioned 230 miles north of Oahu Island. As general commander of the air squadron, I made last-minute checks on

the intelligence information reports in the operations room before going to warm up my single-engine, three-seater "97-type" plane used for level bombing and torpedo flying.

The sunrise in the east was magnificent above the white clouds as I led 360 planes towards Hawaii at an altitude of 3,000 meters. I knew my objective: to surprise and cripple the American naval force in the Pacific. But I fretted about being thwarted should some of the U.S. battleships not be there. I gave no thought of the possibility of this attack breaking open a mortal confrontation with the United States. I was only concerned about making a military success.

As we neared the Hawaiian Islands that bright Sunday morning, I made a preliminary check of the harbor, nearby Hickam Field and the other installations surrounding Honolulu. Viewing the entire American Pacific Fleet peacefully at anchor in the inlet below, I smiled as I reached for the mike and ordered, "All squadrons, plunge in to attack!" The time was 7:49 a.m.

Like a hurricane out of nowhere, my torpedo planes, dive bombers and fighters struck suddenly with indescribable fury. As smoke began to billow and the proud battleships, one by one, started tilting, my heart was almost ablaze with joy. During the next three hours, I directly commanded the fifty level bombers as they pelted not only Pearl Harbor, but the airfields, barracks and dry docks nearby. Then I circled at a higher altitude to accurately assess the damage and report it to my superiors.

Of the eight battleships in the harbor, five were mauled into total inactivity for the time being...Other smaller ships were damaged, but the sting of 3,077 U.S. Navy personnel killed or missing and 876 wounded, plus 226 Army killed and 396 wounded, was something which could never be repaired.

It was the most thrilling exploit of my career.

During the next four years, I was determined to improve upon my Pearl Harbor feat. I saw action in the Solomon Islands, Java, the Indian Ocean; just before the Battle of Midway on June 4, 1942, I came down with an attack of appendicitis and was unable to fly. Lying in my bed, I grimaced at the sounds of the firing all about me. By the end of that day, we had suffered our first major defeat, losing ten warships altogether.

From that time on, things got worse. I did not want to surrender. I would rather have fought to the last man. However, when the Emperor announced that we would surrender, I acquiesced.

I was in Hiroshima the day before the atom bomb was dropped, attending a week long military conference with the Army. Fortunately, I received a long distance call from my Navy Headquarters, asking me to return to Tokyo.

With the end of the war, my military career was over, since all Japanese forces were disbanded. I returned to my home village near Osaka and began farming, but it was a discouraging life. I became more and more unhappy, especially when the war crime trials opened in Tokyo. Though I was never accused, Gen. Douglas MacArthur summoned me to testify on several occasions.

As I got off the train one day in Tokyo's Shibuya Station, I saw an American distributing literature. When I passed him, he handed me a pamphlet entitled I Was a Prisoner of Japan (published by Bible Literature International, known then as the Bible Meditation League). Involved right then with the trials on atrocities committed against war prisoners, I took it.

What I read was the fascinating episode, which eventually changed my life. On that Sunday while I was in the air over Pearl Harbor, an

American soldier named Jake DeShazer had been on K.P. duty in an Army camp in California. When the radio announced the sneak demolishing of Pearl Harbor, he hurled a potato at the wall and shouted, "Jap, just wait and see what we'll do to you!"

One month later, he volunteered for a secret mission with the Jimmy Doolittle Squadron -- a surprise raid on Tokyo from the carrier Hornet. On April 18,1942, DeShazer was one of the bombardiers, and was filled with elation at getting his revenge. After the bombing raid, they flew on towards China, but ran out of fuel and were forced to parachute into Japanese-held territory. The next morning, DeShazer found himself a prisoner of Japan.

During the next forty long months in confinement, DeShazer was cruelly treated. He recalls that his violent hatred for the maltreating Japanese guards almost drove him insane at one point. But after twenty-five months there in Nanking, China, the U.S. prisoners were given a Bible to read. DeShazer, not being an officer, had to let the others use it first. Finally, it came his turn — for three weeks. There in the Japanese P.O.W. camp, he read and read and eventually came to understand that the book was more than an historical classic. Its message became relevant to him right there in his cell.

The dynamic power of Christ, which Jake DeShazer accepted into his life changed his entire attitude toward his captors. His hatred turned to love and concern, and he resolved that should his country win the war and he be liberated, he would someday return to Japan to introduce others to this life-changing book.

DeShazer did just that. After some training at Seattle Pacific College, he returned to Japan as a missionary. And his story, printed in pamphlet form, was something I could not explain.

Neither could I forget it. The peaceful motivation I had read about was exactly what I was seeking. Since the American had found it in the Bible, I decided to purchase one myself, despite my traditionally Buddhist heritage.

In the ensuing weeks, I read this book eagerly. I came to the climactic drama—the Crucifixion. I read in Luke 23:34 the prayer of Jesus Christ at His death: "Father, forgive them; for they know not what they do." I was impressed that I was certainly one of those for whom He had prayed. The many men I had killed had been slaughtered in the name of patriotism, for I did not understand the love which Christ wishes to implant within every heart.

Right at that moment, I seemed to meet Jesus for the first time. I understood the meaning of His death as a substitute for my wickedness, and so in prayer, I requested Him to forgive my sins and change me from a bitter, disillusioned ex-pilot into a well-balanced Christian with purpose in living.

That date, April 14, 1950—became the second "day to remember" of my life. On that day, I became a new person. My complete view on life was changed by the intervention of the Christ I had always hated and ignored before. Soon other friends beyond my close family learned of my decision to be a follower of Christ, and they could hardly understand it.

Big headlines appeared in the papers: "Pearl Harbor Hero Converts to Christianity." Old war buddies came to visit me, trying to persuade me to discard "this crazy idea." Others accused me of being an opportunist, embracing Christianity only for how it might impress our American victors.

But time has proven them wrong. As an evangelist, I have traveled across Japan and the Orient introducing others to the One Who changed my life. I believe with all my heart that those who will direct Japan—and all other nations—in the decades to come must not ignore the message of Jesus Christ. Youth must realize that He is the only hope for this troubled world.

Though my country has the highest literacy rate in the world, education has not brought salvation. Peace and freedom—both national and personal—come only through an encounter with Jesus Christ.

I would give anything to retract my actions of twenty-nine years ago at Pearl Harbor, but it is impossible. Instead, I now work at striking the death-blow to the basic hatred which infests the human heart and causes such tragedies. And that hatred cannot be uprooted without assistance from Jesus Christ.

He is the only One Who was powerful enough to change my life and inspire it with His thoughts. He was the only answer to Jake DeShazer's tormented life. He is the only answer for young people today."[14]

Tracts work! For more information about where to get some to hand out, you can go to www.markcahill.org.

Public parks, beaches, the bar section of towns, and festivals are all good places to go out and be watchmen.

I was witnessing in the bar section of town once, and I stopped and looked around at all the partying and people who were drunk and throwing their lives away, and I said to myself, "And Mark Cahill, you used to think this was fun." It really amazed me to think how deceived I had been by the enemy. But that is also what drives me to go back out there and reach these people for Jesus Christ before it is too late.

I received this email recently:

"In my early college years, I was being pursued by the Lord in many ways. One of those ways was on a night of bar hopping and drinking with friends, when Mark Cahill walked up and started to witness to me. I had grown up in church, but was far away from my Christian roots at the time. I remember listening to what he had to say with a bit of confusion due to the alcohol level in my system, but one thing did translate; that God loved me and wanted me for His own. My friend and I got in the car that night and cried all the way home out of pure sorrow for how we were living our lives, then spoke to one another (this time sober) a couple of times about the incident. To make a long story short, I gave my life over to Christ within a few years of that time and now, about 13 years later, I am the wife to a wonderful pastor and we work to share the gospel with this world. The other night, I was reading about the prophet Jeremiah and his statements that he wished he had never been born due to the mocking of the people around him who didn't understand the message the Lord had given him to speak. Yet, the Lord's Words burned like fire within His bones. I thought about the guy named Mark Cahill who obediently walked up to these drunk girls on the street and started to witness to them. It has to seem like such a thankless job to witness to people whose eyes are glazed over with alcohol. It also is one of those jobs that you very seldom see anything but the seed being planted (and in this case, must wonder if it is being planted at all). I was just telling our elder and his wife about this guy who had impacted me in my early 20s and how I still remembered his name. That is what led me to look him up tonight on the computer. Just wanted to let him know that his faithfulness is appreciated and that he truly does practice what he preaches! Thank you for your willingness to go out and share the gospel in the way that you do."

Never forget that you really don't know whom you are talking to. It might look like some drunk ladies, but it might just be a preacher's wife and a soul winner one day! That is also why we as watchmen don't always look for fruit. That evening, I didn't see any fruit with those ladies, but God was not done by a long shot. That is why it is our job to always remain faithful.

Matthew 8:26: "And he saith unto them, Why are ye fearful, O ye of little faith?..."

2 Corinthians 5:7: "(For we walk by faith, not by sight:)"

Matthew 25:23: "His lord said unto him, Well done, good and faithful servant; thou hast been faithful over a few things, I will make thee ruler over many things: enter thou into the joy of thy lord."

But never forget to be soul winners as you go through your daily life. Why not talk to people at a gas station? Once, I stopped at a gas station in Birmingham and struck up a conversation with this couple. I ended up giving them one of my books. They came back over later and said, "Have you written anything else?" I said that I had and mentioned the title. She had read the book when she was in prison, and he was given a copy of the same book by a physical therapist who shares his faith with all of his patients! What a divine appointment that was! But since I pray to go to the right gas station, none of this surprises me anymore. But I have to be honest: It does excite me, because I get to see God's hand moving right in front of my eyes!

Why not talk to people about the Lord at the hotels where you stay? I had a wonderful conversation with Valentina one day at a hotel in Cincinnati. She was Russian. Her grandfather was arrested in Russia for his faith in Jesus Christ and was put in a hard labor camp for two years, because he wouldn't renounce Jesus. Her father saw what happened and didn't want the same persecution, so he didn't want to be a believer. Just to show you how great God is, her dad is now not only a believer but the pastor of a church in Russia! The persecution of her granddad showed her dad how important it was to believe in Jesus no matter the cost. Valentina also had a very strong faith in the Lord and loves to talk about Jesus!

Acts 17:18: "Then certain philosophers of the Epicureans, and of the Stoicks, encountered him. And some said, What will this babbler say?

other some, He seemeth to be a setter forth of strange gods: because he preached unto them Jesus, and the resurrection."

I really don't think Paul was mad at the people. He was mad that they were deceived, and he wanted to do something about it! Do you feel the same way?

Talk about the Resurrection! It is what truly sets Jesus apart from every other religious person that has ever walked on planet earth.

You are gambling on who Jesus is. You best know exactly who He is before you die!

1 Corinthians 15:14: "And if Christ be not risen, then *is* our preaching vain, and your faith *is* also vain."

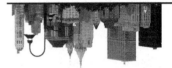

If Jesus did not rise from the dead, this is all one big fairy tale. I had a man tell me one time that even if Jesus didn't rise from the dead, I would still have had a good life. No I wouldn't! I would have wasted it on telling people what was out there when they died, and it wasn't true. I would have believed in Someone that could cleanse me of my sins, and He really couldn't. What a wasted life I would have led. Unless of course, it is true! Then I have hit the jackpot for all of eternity! Don't forget that you are taking an eternal gamble here. You are gambling on who Jesus is. You best know exactly who He is before you die!

Acts 17:19: "And they took him, and brought him unto Areopagus, saying, May we know what this new doctrine, whereof thou speakest, *is*?"

People have questions. We must be ready to answer those questions.

1 Peter 3:15: "But sanctify the Lord God in your hearts: and *be* ready always to *give* an answer to every man that asketh you a reason of the hope that is in you with meekness and fear:"

On a plane one day, the gentleman next to me was an engineer. He had owned four companies and was a real thinker. He just kept firing questions at me: 'How do you know there is a God?' 'How do you know the Bible is true?' etc. Towards the end of the conversation, I said, "Do you have any more questions for me?" He said, "No, you have answered everything I have thrown at you!" I am so glad I take time to study what I believe and practice sharing my faith.

Then I told him that I always pray for the person that sits next to me on plane flights and that we were supposed to be sitting next to each other. He looked at me and said, "I am not supposed to be on this flight!" When he was coming through the Orlando airport earlier that morning, he had a box of bullets in his carry-on bag! A friend had given them to him a month earlier, he threw them in a bag, and that just happened to be the one he brought to the airport. He said that he ended up having to talk to the police, and the FBI, which delayed him and he had to take the next flight to Atlanta, and that was how we were next to each other. I said to him, "I prayed for whoever would sit next to me, but I had nothing to do with the bullets in your bag!"

Acts 17:20 "For thou bringest certain strange things to our ears: we would know therefore what these things mean."

As I said earlier, it's very important to use God's Law with people. Sin isn't a strange thing. People have a conscience, and they know they have broken those commandments, so that is something that is familiar to them.

Hebrews 4:13: "Neither is there any creature that is not manifest in his sight: but all things *are* naked and opened unto the eyes of him with whom we have to do."

Nothing will catch us by surprise on Judgment Day, and nothing will catch God by surprise on that day either! Never forget, though, that this verse is a verse of caring. God cares about every single little detail in our lives! What a loving Creator we serve!

> **Acts 17:21:** "(For all the Athenians and strangers which were there spent their time in nothing else, but either to tell, or to hear some new thing.)"

Nothing will catch us by surprise on Judgment Day, and nothing will catch God by surprise on that day either!

People like to talk, so get them talking about some subject. The more you chat with someone, the more it builds the friendship between you. When you begin to drop a serious question into the conversation, they already like you, so most of the time they will continue the conversation.

> **Acts 17:22:** "Then Paul stood in the midst of Mars' hill, and said, *Ye* men of Athens, I perceive that in all things ye are too superstitious."

'Superstitious' means religious in this context, or worshipping false gods. We see that everywhere we go in our culture.

> **Acts 17:23:** "For as I passed by, and beheld your devotions, I found an altar with this inscription, TO THE UNKNOWN GOD. Whom therefore ye ignorantly worship, him declare I unto you."

You see they had the trappings of religion. They had all of their bases covered. Even if they worshipped the wrong god, they still had a statue to the Unknown God, just in case he is the one they would stand in front of on Judgment Day!

In a hotel one day, I met the owner, who was Hindu. He had statues for Brahman, Vishnu, Jesus–he had all of his bases covered! Just in case one of those gods was out there when he died, he could say that he had bowed down and worshipped him at some point.

So remember like I've taught you, use things around you to get into conversations. Use inscriptions on buildings, t-shirts, hats, jewelry, tattoos, or bracelets. Any of those things are a great segue into a spiritual conversation.

> **Acts 17:24:** "God that made the world and all things therein, seeing that he is Lord of heaven and earth, dwelleth not in temples made with hands;"

God has made it all! This is a very important foundation that must be laid. People have heard too many times that there is no God, and that we have all just evolved from animals. Biblical creation matters! The book of Genesis matters!

> **Acts 17:25, 26:** "Neither is worshipped with men's hands, as though he needed any thing, seeing he giveth to all life, and breath, and all things; And hath made of one blood all nations of men for to dwell on all the face of the earth, and hath determined the times before appointed, and the bounds of their habitation;"

God is the only One who gives us breath. He holds our breath in the palm of His hand, according to Daniel. We should be so thankful. We should be so grateful. We should want to cherish those breaths and speak words of eternal life into others.

And never forget that God said we are of one blood. And since we are all of one blood, there should never be a hint of racism in you. A Christian cannot entertain racist thoughts. We entertain Godly thoughts!

> **Revelation 7:9:** "After this I beheld, and, lo, a great multitude, which no man could number, of all nations, and kindreds, and people, and tongues, stood before the throne, and before the Lamb, clothed with white robes, and palms in their hands;"

It is going to be a beautiful day before the throne with such an array of different people! As I always tell people, if all of your friends look just like you, you have a problem! Heaven will be nothing like that. If you do not have friends of different races, today is the day to change that!

> **Acts 17:27:** "That they should seek the Lord, if haply they might feel after him, and find him, though he be not far from every one of us:"

God is not far from anyone. All they have to do is repent and believe. Some Christians think certain lost people are so far from the Lord that there is no way they can be saved.

I have received four or five letters from David Berkowitz. He was the Son of Sam killer in New York back in the 70s. He repented of his sins and became born again! He has run the chapel in his prison for 25 years. The guards will talk about

People are made to worship. If we don't worship the God of the Bible, we will worship someone or something.

how there has been a true conversion. He cried out to God in his jail cell and God answered! The Most High God is not far from anyone of us!

> **Acts 17:28, 29:** "For in him we live, and move, and have our being; as certain also of your own poets have said, For we are also his offspring. Forasmuch then as we are the offspring of God, we ought not to think that the Godhead is like unto gold, or silver, or stone, graven by art and man's device."

People are made to worship. If we don't worship the God of the Bible, we will worship someone or something.

Every four years, what do we see people chasing on our televisions? Gold, silver, and bronze medals. Some people will spend countless hours and literally their entire lifetime trying to get one of those medals.

Years ago, I played college basketball with Charles Barkley at Auburn. Years later, as adults, I was at his house in

Phoenix, and he had this case on the wall with a picture of the United States Dream Team and the gold medal they had won at the Olympics draped around it. So I was looking at it, and I called Charles over and said, "Is this it? Is this all it is?" I was dumbfounded at how small that medal was. I don't know what I was expecting, but that sure wasn't it. I must have been expecting something like one of those big rapper's medals or something!

Once when I was still teaching, an Olympic diver came to the school to speak to the students. She walked down the aisles, opened a case with her bronze medal in it and would ask people: "Would you like to touch my medal?" The idol worship of the medal was amazing, and it wasn't even a gold medal!

Remember to worship God and Him alone, and you will be just fine.

Acts 17:30: "And the times of this ignorance God winked at; but now commandeth all men every where to repent:"

God is winking no more at the ignorance of this world. He is commanding people to biblical repentance. Christianity is not some 'get out of hell free card.' This is very, very serious business. People's eternal lives are on the line. Let's take this as seriously as we should be.

Acts 17:31: "Because he hath appointed a day, in the which he will judge the world in righteousness by *that* man whom he hath ordained; *whereof* he hath given assurance unto all *men*, in that he hath raised him from the dead."

Again, Paul is emphasizing how important the resurrection is. One thing I tell people is, "Since Jesus rose from the dead, so will you!" It is a good seed to plant in people's lives. I want them to realize that even though they think people are dead, those people are really still alive.

Daniel 12:2: "And many of them that sleep in the dust of the earth shall awake, some to everlasting life, and some to shame *and* everlasting contempt."

Acts 17:32-34: "And when they heard of the resurrection of the dead, some mocked: and others said, We will hear thee again of this *matter*. So Paul departed from among them. Howbeit certain men clave unto him, and believed: among the which *was* Dionysius the Areopagite, and a woman named Damaris, and others with them."

Some people may mock when they hear about the eternal truths of God. They may mock the resurrection. But a watchman always knows that he is not in the business of pleasing people. A watchman knows everyone isn't going to like him, and a watchman is okay with that. The souls of the lost are too important to the watchman.

Mission trips are tons of fun, but we cannot forget about the souls that are around us every day. When I was speaking at Biola University one time in Los Angeles, I asked the students how they could care about the souls in Venezuela, if they didn't care about the souls on Venice Beach! I found out later there was an 80-year-old missionary there that was stomping his feet with joy to hear that! He knew that all souls matter to God.

Watchmen are in the business of turning this world upside down. They know that is why they are here.

Watchmen are in the business of turning this world upside down. They know that is why they are here. They will take the gospel message wherever it is needed. They follow the likes of Paul here in Acts. Watchmen: Take the gospel to your streets, and do it now!

The Bible is not a buffet from which we can pick and choose what we want to believe or what fits our thinking.

Chapter 8
Is Not My Word as Like a Fire?

"We are raising a generation on the spiritual junk food of religious videos, movies, youth entertainment, and comic book paraphrases of the Bible. The Word of God is being rewritten, watered down, illustrated, and dramatized in order to cater to the taste of the carnal mind. That only leads further into the wilderness of doubt and confusion."[15]
–Dave Hunt

One thing a watchman always knows is that he or she must herald the right truths. There are lies everywhere. If we do not proclaim truth in this culture; if we do not proclaim the right path for people to take; if we do not proclaim the Biblical Jesus; there is no hope for anyone. It is literally that simple.

And of course, the watchman always knows that the source of his proclamations is the Word of God! And once you have a right view of the Bible, it can change everything!

....

"Suppose a nation in some distant region should take the Bible for their only law Book, and every member should regulate his conduct by the precepts there exhibited! Every member would be obliged in conscience, to temperance, frugality, and industry; to justice, kindness, and charity towards his fellow men; and to piety, love, and reverence toward Almighty God...what a Utopia, what a Paradise would this region be."[16]
–John Adams

....

"So great is my veneration for the Bible that the earlier my children begin to read it,

the more confident will be my hope that they will prove useful citizens to their country and respectable members of society."

"I have made it a practice for several years to read the Bible through in the course of every year. I usually devote to this reading the first hour after I rise every morning..."[17]
–JOHN QUINCY ADAMS

....

"The Bible is God's chart for you to steer by, to keep you from the bottom of the sea, and to show you where the harbour is, and how to reach it without running on rocks and bars."[18]
–HENRY WARD BEECHER

....

"The secret of my success? It is simple. It is found in the Bible, 'In all thy ways acknowledge Him and He shall direct thy paths.'"[19]
–GEORGE WASHINGTON CARVER

....

"The Bible – banned, burned, beloved. More widely read, more frequently attacked than any other book in history. Generations of intellectuals have attempted to discredit it, dictators of every age have outlawed it and executed those who read it. Yet soldiers carry it into battle believing it more powerful than their weapons. Fragments of it smuggled into solitary prison cells have transformed ruthless killers into gentle saints."[20]
–CHARLES COLSON

"Do you know a book that you are willing to put under your head for a pillow when you are dying? Very well; that is the Book you want to study when you are living. There is only one such Book in the world."[21]

–Joseph Cook

"After more than sixty years of almost daily reading of the Bible, I never fail to find it always new and marvelously in tune with the changing needs of every day."[22]

–Cecil B. DeMille

"To what greater inspiration and counsel can we turn than to the imperishable truth to be found in this Treasure House, the Bible?"[23]

–Queen Elizabeth

"There is a Book worth all other books which were ever printed."[24]

–Patrick Henry

"The Bible is the Rock upon which this Republic rests."[25]

–Andrew Jackson

"A studious persual of the sacred volume will make better citizens, better fathers, and better husbands."[26]

–Thomas Jefferson

"The Bible gives me a deep, comforting sense that 'things seen are temporal, and things unseen are eternal.'"[27]

–HELEN KELLER

"The Bible is a Book in comparison with which all others are of minor importance, and which in all my perplexities and distresses has never failed to give me light and strength."[28]

–ROBERT E. LEE

"Without Divine assistance I cannot succeed; With it I cannot fail!"

"I believe the Bible is the best gift God has ever given to man. All the good of the Savior of the world is communicated to us through the Book. But for it, we could not know right from wrong?"[29]

–ABRAHAM LINCOLN

"Western literature has been more influenced by the Bible than any other book."[30]

–THOMAS B. MACAULAY

"The book to read is not one which thinks for you, but the one that makes you think. No other book in the world equals the Bible for that."[31]

–JAMES MCCOSH

"Sin will keep you from this Book. This Book will keep you from sin."[32]
—D.L. Moody

"I consider an intimate knowledge of the Bible an indispensable quality of a well educated man."[33]
—Dr. Robert Milikan

"There's far more truth in the Book of Genesis than in the quantum theory."[34]
—Malcolm Muggeridge

"The Bible is not merely a book; it is a Living Being, with an action, a power, which invades everything that opposes its extension, behold! It is upon this table: This Book, surpassing all others; I never omit to read it, and every day with some pleasure."[35]
—Napoleon

"There are more sure marks of authenticity in the Bible than in any profane history. I have a fundamental belief in the Bible as the Word of God, written by men who were inspired. I study the Bible daily."[36]
—Sir Isaac Newton

"This little Book [The Bible]—it has said everything there is to be said. Everything is implied and anticipated in it. Whatever one should like to put into words has already been

said in it."[37]
—MORDECAI OBADIAH

....

"The Bible is still loved by millions, read by millions, and studied by millions."

"Jews preserved it [God's Holy Scriptures] as no other manuscript has ever been preserved. With their Massora, they kept tabs on every letter, syllable, word and paragraph. They had special classes of men within their culture whose sole duty was to preserve and transmit these documents with practically perfect fidelity—scribes, lawyers, massorettes."[38]
—BERNARD RAMM

....

"Of the many influences that have shaped the United States into a distinctive nation and people, none may be said to be more fundamental and enduring than the Bible."[39]
—RONALD REAGAN

....

"It is necessary for the welfare of the nation that men's lives be based on the principles of the Bible. No man, educated or uneducated, can afford to be ignorant of the Bible."

"A thorough understanding of the Bible is better than a college education."[40]
—THEODORE ROOSEVELT

....

"The Bible is superior to all other religious books in content. It sets up the highest ethical standards, enjoins the most absolute obedience, denounces every form of sin, and yet informs the sinner how he can become right with God. How could uninspired men write a book like that?"[41]

–Henry Thiessen

"The Bible is the only Book by which you may know certainly the future; It is the only Book that satisfactorily answers the questions, 'Where did I come from? Why am I here? Where am I going?'"[42]

–Anonymous

"I have read many books, but the Bible reads me."[43]

–Anonymous

"Tell your prince that this Book (the Bible) is the secret of England's greatness."[44]

–Queen Victoria (to an African prince)

"It is impossible to rightly govern the world without God and the Bible."[45]

–George Washington

"If there is anything in my thoughts or style to commend, the credit is due my parents for instilling in me an early love of the Scriptures. If we abide by the principles taught in the Bible, our country will go on prospering and to prosper; but if we and our posterity neglect its instructions and authority, no man can tell how sudden a catastrophe may overwhelm us and bury all our glory in profound obscurity."

"The Bible fits man for life and prepares him for death."

"Education is useless without the Bible."[46]
–DANIEL WEBSTER

....

"This Book [the Bible] had to be written by one of three people: good men, bad men or God. It couldn't have been written by good men, because they said it was inspired by the revelation of God. Good men don't lie and deceive. It couldn't have been written by bad men, because bad men would not write something that would condemn themselves. It leaves only one conclusion. It was given by divine inspiration of God."

"I am a Bible-bigot. I follow it in all things, both great and small."[47]
–JOHN WESLEY

....

"I am sorry for men who do not read the Bible every day. I wonder why they deprive themselves of the strength and pleasure."

"A man has deprived himself of the best there is in the world who has deprived himself of this knowledge of the Bible."[48]
–WOODROW WILSON

A watchman always knows the importance of God's Word. He understands that the Bible belongs on the top shelf of his book collection, and no other book really even belongs in the bookcase. But a Bible on the top shelf that collects dust is no good at all. A Bible that is well-worn and studied and obeyed is God's kind of Bible!

A Bible on the top shelf that collects dust is no good at all. A Bible that is well-worn and studied and obeyed is God's kind of Bible!

2 Timothy 3:14-17: "But continue thou in the things which thou hast learned and hast been assured of, knowing of whom thou hast learned *them*; And that from a child thou hast known the holy scriptures, which are able to make thee wise unto salvation through faith which is in Christ Jesus. All scripture *is* given by inspiration of God, and *is* profitable for doctrine, for reproof, for correction, for instruction in righteousness: That the man of God may be perfect, throughly furnished unto all good works."

God has breathed all of His Scripture into existence. The Bible can be read and learned by a child. This book needs to be spoken into the lives of children. The first book they should ever learn to read is God's Word. Be very careful about putting picture Bibles in front of kids. They might get enraptured with the pictures and not the script on the page. Satan may also trick them into thinking it is just a storybook instead of a book of real accounts of real people. Jesus didn't have a picture Bible as a kid, and He turned out just fine. Instill that Word of God into those children at a very young age.

2 Peter 1:18, 19: "And this voice which came from heaven we heard, when we were with him in the holy mount. We have also a more sure word of prophecy; whereunto ye do well that ye take heed, as unto a light that shineth in a dark place, until the day dawn, and the day star arise in your hearts:"

One beautiful aspect of the Bible is that it speaks to you right where you are. It will pierce your soul with truth.

The Scriptures are the sure Word of Prophecy that you have in your hands. It will be the light that will guide you in the darkness of this world.

Hebrews 4:12: "For the word of God *is* quick, and powerful, and sharper than any twoedged sword, piercing even to the dividing asunder of soul and spirit, and of the joints and marrow, and *is a* discerner of the thoughts and intents of the heart."

One beautiful aspect of the Bible is that it speaks to you right where you are. It will pierce your soul with truth. It will convict. It is always good to ask people the question, "Do you read the Bible?" It is important to get lost people to read that Book.

Back in the day before I was saved, I had a coworker that was committing adultery. He was a Christian. He told me that when he read the Bible, almost every verse he read was about adultery. Now even though I wasn't saved, I still had a little common sense and I said, "I get the feeling you've read all of those verses before, but they had no meaning to you then." That is the power of the Word of God. Very shortly after that, he repented of his sins, because God's words convicted him that is not how you treat your wife and that is not how you treat God.

Revelation 22:18, 19: "For I testify unto every man that heareth the words of the prophecy of this book, If any man shall add unto these things, God shall add unto him the plagues that are written in this book: And if any man shall take away from the words of the book of this prophecy, God shall take away his part out of the book of life, and out of the holy city, and *from* the things which are written in this book."

God takes his Word very seriously. You don't mess with His Word. You don't add the Book of Mormon to it, the Pearl of Great Price, the Koran, or the Hadith. You have the complete package in the Holy Bible.

Proverbs 30:5, 6: "Every word of God *is* pure: he *is* a shield unto them that put their trust in him. Add thou not unto his words, lest he reprove thee, and thou be found a liar."

Luke 11:27, 28: "And it came to pass, as he spake these things, a certain woman of the company lifted up her voice, and said unto him, Blessed *is* the womb that bare thee, and the paps which thou hast sucked. But he said, Yea rather, blessed *are* they that hear the word of God, and keep it."

Obedience is a key part of the Christian walk. You will read a lot of Scripture in this book. 'Read and heed,' as one of my friends says. Keep God's Word all the days of your life!

Revelation 6:9: "And when he had opened the fifth seal, I saw under the altar the souls of them that were slain for the word of God, and for the testimony which they held:"

Would you be willing to die for the Word of God?

2 Timothy 2:9: "Wherein I suffer trouble, as an evil doer, *even* unto bonds; but the word of God is not bound."

I was just reading an email from a friend who told me that a 14-year-old boy was arrested in China for handing out gospel tracts. Would you be willing to give up part of your life fulfilling a jail sentence, or your whole life by dying for sharing God's words with the lost?

Joshua 1:7-9: "Only be thou strong and very courageous, that thou mayest observe to do according to all the law, which Moses my servant commanded thee: turn not from it *to* the right hand or *to* the left, that thou mayest prosper whithersoever thou goest. This book of the law shall not depart out of thy mouth; but thou shalt meditate therein day and night, that thou mayest observe to do according to all that is written therein:

You cannot be the follower of God that you want to be without a thorough understanding of God's Word. If you do not soak your mind in His Word, your growth will be stunted.

for then thou shalt make thy way prosperous, and then thou shalt have good success. Have not I commanded thee? Be strong and of a good courage; be not afraid, neither be thou dismayed: for the LORD thy God *is* with thee whithersoever thou goest."

As a watchman, do you meditate on God's Word? Do you have those verses rolling through your head as you wait for battle? Do you have them in your head as the battle takes place?

1 Peter 2:2: "As newborn babes, desire the sincere milk of the word, that ye may grow thereby."

You cannot be the follower of God that you want to be without a thorough understanding of God's Word. If you do not soak your mind in His Word, your growth will be stunted. If you don't eat the right foods, drink water, and breathe enough air, you will die physically, and the same is true spiritually. Without a healthy diet of God's Word, you will waste away into a frail representation of what a Christian really is.

Mark 7:7, 8: "Howbeit in vain do they worship me, teaching *for* doctrines the commandments of men. For laying aside the commandment of God, ye hold the tradition of men, as the washing of pots and cups: and many other such like things ye do."

Men's opinions or God's truths: Which one are you going to follow?

2 Timothy 4:2, 3: "Preach the word; be instant in season, out of season; reprove, rebuke, exhort with all longsuffering and doctrine. For the time will come when they will not endure sound doctrine; but after their own lusts shall they heap to themselves teachers, having itching ears;"

I was speaking at a church in Wichita one time, and the pastor left a gift basket for me. With it was a card, which simply said: "Preach the word!" I read a study that said forty percent of all pastors don't feel comfortable preaching absolute truth to their congregations. If that is a true statistic, either those pastors need to step down from their pulpit and no longer be preachers, or they need to stop fearing what men might say or do. Watchmen can't worry about everyone's feelings or if someone might stop donating to the cause. They always do what is right.

> **Proverbs 2:1-6:** "My son, if thou wilt receive my words, and hide my commandments with thee; So that thou incline thine ear unto wisdom, *and* apply thine heart to understanding; Yea, if thou criest after knowledge, *and* liftest up thy voice for understanding; If thou seekest her as silver, and searchest *for* her as for hid treasures; Then shalt thou understand the fear of the LORD, and find the knowledge of God. For the LORD giveth wisdom: out of his mouth *cometh* knowledge and understanding."

People travelled all across America to get to the West Coast for the Gold Rush, but would you walk two steps over to your bookcase and crack open the eternal Word of God which is more precious than gold?

> **Psalm 119:9-11:** "Wherewithal shall a young man cleanse his way? By taking heed *thereto* according to thy word. With my whole heart have I sought thee: O let me not wander from thy commandments. Thy word have I hid in mine heart, that I might not sin against thee."

We hide our treasures, so no one can steal them. Have you hidden God's Word in your heart so that you won't sin against Him and even if someone stole your Bible, His treasures would still be safe inside your heart and memory?

> **Psalm 119:89:** "For ever, O LORD, thy word is settled in heaven."

One thing a watchman does is always point people to the Word of God. Why? It is already settled in heaven. You can argue against it all you want to, but those truths are eternal, and they will never change! That is why it is a joy to stand upon God's Word, because it is a rock that will never be moved!

Psalm 119:97-105: "O how love I thy law! It *is* my meditation all the day. Thou through thy commandments hast made me wiser than mine enemies: for they *are* ever with me. I have more understanding than all my teachers: for thy testimonies *are* my meditation. I understand more than the ancients, because I keep thy precepts. I have refrained my feet from every evil way, that I might keep thy word. I have not departed from thy judgments: for thou hast taught me. How sweet are thy words unto my taste! *yea, sweeter* than honey to my mouth! Through thy precepts I get understanding: therefore I hate every false way. Thy word is a lamp unto my feet, and a light unto my path."

It is so nice to have something that tastes so good on our taste buds. We will travel to our favorite restaurant just to have one of those wonderful meals. Do you feel the same way about the Word of God? That you just can't wait to open it to taste and see what the Lord has for you today!

2 Timothy 2:15: "Study to shew thyself approved unto God, a workman that needeth not to be ashamed, rightly dividing the word of truth."

The word 'study' means to exert oneself or to give effort towards. We will wear ourselves out training to play a sport or studying for a final exam, but do you ever wear yourself out studying God's Word?

1 Peter 1:24, 25: "For all flesh *is* as grass, and all the glory of man as the flower of grass. The grass withereth, and the flower thereof falleth away: But the word of the Lord endureth for ever. And this is the word which by the gospel is preached unto you."

God's words have an eternal quality to them. They shall last forever. We all might as well soak our minds with words that will last for eternity, rather than with so many words that won't!

Never forget that three things will last for eternity: The triune God, His words, and people's souls. And all three of those will always matter to a watchman!

Never forget that three things will last for eternity: The triune God, His words, and people's souls. And all three of those will always matter to a watchman!

One of the real dangers for the watchman is false doctrine. Satan will try and get some doctrine stuck inside of you to get you off of the narrow road. He doesn't care how it happens. He doesn't care who teaches it to you. He doesn't care in what book you read it. He just wants you off of the narrow road; and once off that road, he wants you to stay off of it for a long time.

That is why we always teach people to keep their guard up–So you can protect yourself against false teachings. You must take everything you hear, and filter it against the Word of God. If it doesn't agree with the Word of God, throw it to the wayside. Get it out of your way quickly, before the enemy can get a foothold with those false teachings.

Many people are teaching now that there are many paths to heaven; that Jesus isn't the only way to get there.

Reverend Gene Robinson, the openly gay Episcopal Bishop of New Hampshire, said at the opening inaugural event for Barack Obama:

> "Welcome to Washington! The fun is about to begin, but first, please join me in pausing for a moment, to ask God's blessing upon our nation and our next president: 'O God of our many understandings, we pray that you will…'[49]

When people talk about the 'God of our many under-standings,' what is the implication?

In his prayer at President Obama's inauguration, Rick Warren said:

> "I humbly ask this in the name of the One Who changed my life – Yeshua, Isa, Jesus, [Spanish pronunciation], Jesus – who taught us to pray…:"[50]

'Yeshua' is the Hebraic form of Jesus–a language that is mostly spoken by people of the Jewish belief. 'Isa' is the Arabic form of Jesus–a language that is mostly spoken by people who are Muslim. The name 'Jesus' pronounced in Spanish–a language that is mostly spoken by people who are Roman Catholic. In a simple prayer, Mr. Warren decided to put all of these religions under the same umbrella by using the name of Jesus in different ways. Is that the correct thing to do?

Barack Obama said in an interview with Cathleen Falsani,

> "So, I'm rooted in the Christian tradition. I believe that there are many paths to the same place, and that is a belief that there is a high-er power, a belief that we are connected as a people."[51]

So is President Obama correct in his belief that there are many paths to the same place?

Pope John Paul II said,

> "It will be in the sincere practice of what is good in their own reli-gious traditions and by following the dictates of their own conscience that the members of other religions respond positively to God's invi-tation and receive salvation in Jesus Christ, even while they do not recognize him or acknowledge him as their savior."[52]

How can someone receive salvation in Jesus Christ if they do not acknowledge Him as Savior?

Billy Graham said,

> "I used to believe that pagans in far off countries were lost, were going to hell. I no longer believe that. I believe that there are other ways of recognizing the existence of God."[53]

So are there other ways to recognize God's existence, or is there just one way?

President Bush said in an interview with Cynthia McFadden,

"I do believe there is an Almighty that is broad and big enough, loving enough that can encompass a lot of people. I don't think God is a narrow concept. I think it's a broad concept. I just happen to believe the way to God is through Christ, and others have different avenues toward God, and I believe we pray to the same Almighty. I do."[54]

Matthew 7:13, 14: "Enter ye in at the strait gate: for wide *is* the gate, and broad *is* the way, that leadeth to destruction, and many there be which go in thereat: Because strait *is* the gate, and narrow *is* the way, which leadeth unto life, and few there be that find it."

So which is it? Is Jesus correct that it is a narrow road, or is President Bush in saying that it is a broad way?

In the fictional book *The Shack*, Paul Young wrote that Jesus says,

"I am the best way any human can relate to Papa or Sarayu."[55]

So is Jesus the best way to relate to the Father in heaven or the only way?

So watchmen, where do we look to find the correct answer? We always go to the Word of God!

John 14:6: "Jesus saith unto him, I am the way, the truth, and the life: no man cometh unto the Father, but by me."

Acts 4:12: "Neither is there salvation in any other: for there is none other name under heaven given among men, whereby we must be saved."

Acts 16:30, 31: "And brought them out, and said, Sirs, what must I do to be saved? And they said, Believe on the Lord Jesus Christ, and thou shalt be saved, and thy house."

1 Timothy 2:5: "For *there is* one God, and one mediator between God and men, the man Christ Jesus;"

1 John 2:23: "Whosoever denieth the Son, the same hath not the Father: *(but) he that acknowledgeth the Son hath the Father also.*"

1 John 5:11, 12: "And this is the record, that God hath given to us eternal life, and this life is in his Son. "He that hath the Son hath life; and he that hath not the Son of God hath not life."

John 3:16: "For God so loved the world, that he gave his only begotten Son, that whosoever believeth in him should not perish, but have everlasting life."

John 3:36: "He that believeth on the Son hath everlasting life: and he that believeth not the Son shall not see life; but the wrath of God abideth on him."

John 8:24: "I said therefore unto you, that ye shall die in your sins: for if ye believe not that I am *he*, ye shall die in your sins."

Those verses really do clear it up, don't they? I really think what all this comes down to is feelings. Some folks don't want to offend anyone. They don't want to offend a person by saying their belief system is incorrect. But how can it be offensive to tell someone the truth? As a matter of fact, the most loving thing you can ever do is tell someone the truth!

You must also understand that the Bible promises that there will be other gospels being preached in this world.

Galatians 1:6-9: "I marvel that ye are so soon removed from him that called you into the grace of Christ unto another gospel: Which is not another; but there be some that trouble you, and would pervert the gospel of Christ. But though we, or an angel from heaven, preach any other gospel unto you than that which we have preached unto you, let him be accursed. As we said before, so say I now again, If any *man* preach any other gospel unto you than that ye have received, let him be accursed."

The word 'accursed' means something that has a curse upon it and cannot be redeemed. That is a very serious word. God is not playing here. If you play around with His Gospel, you are messing with His Son. And you can rest assured *that God will take that seriously.*

> **2 Corinthians 11:4:** "For if he that cometh preacheth another Jesus, whom we have not preached, or *if* ye receive another spirit, which ye have not received, or another gospel, which ye have not accepted, ye might well bear with *him.*"

God says this one more time in 2 Corinthians. He really doesn't want you to miss the point. There is only one Gospel and only one way to the Father, and that is through Jesus Christ.

*The word 'accursed' means something that has a curse upon it and cannot be redeemed. That is a very serious word. God is not playing here. If you play around with His Gospel, you are messing with His Son. And you can rest assured **that God will take that seriously**.*

> **Galatians 1:10:** "For do I now persuade men, or God? or do I seek to please men? for if I yet pleased men, I should not be the servant of Christ."

Watchmen can never be concerned what others think about them. We must point out false teachings, so others will not be deceived about eternity. Pleasing men isn't an option for a watchman.

> **John 17:3:** "And this is life eternal, that they might know thee the only true God, and Jesus Christ, whom thou hast sent."

The truth of the matter is when you question whether Jesus is the only way to heaven, you are really questioning God's Word. Is the Bible the inerrant Word of God or not?

> **2 Peter 1:20, 21:** "Knowing this first, that no prophecy of the scripture is of any private interpretation. For the prophecy came not in

old time by the will of man: but holy men of God spake *as they were* moved by the Holy Ghost."

We know from historical accounts, archaeology, and fulfilled prophecy that the Bible is the holy book that you can rest your eternal soul upon. All religions come down to a book or books. The Bible is the only one that has been proven throughout history to be accurate and true.

Psalm 12:6: "The words of the LORD *are* pure words: *as* silver tried in a furnace of earth, purified seven times."

God's words have been tested, and they are pure!

Psalm 19:7: "The law of the LORD *is* perfect, converting the soul: the testimony of the LORD *is* sure, making wise the simple."

We know that God's scriptures are perfect, and we use His Law and His words as we make our stand for Him!

Lots of people wonder, "Who is Jesus?" I was talking with a woman named Deborah in the mall once, and she said, "Do you really think Jesus is God?" As we continued our conversation, I found out that she had grown up Jehovah's Witness. She was taught that Jesus was the archangel Michael. She had recently been kicked out of the Jehovah's Witness church.

John 1:1: "In the beginning was the Word, and the Word was with God, and the Word was God."

John 1:14: "And the Word was made flesh, and dwelt among us, (and we beheld his glory, the glory as of the only begotten of the Father,) full of grace and truth."

It is very obvious by looking at the Gospel of John, that Jesus is the Word and the Word was God! Yes, Jesus is God!

1 John 5:7: "For there are three that bear record in heaven, the Father, the Word, and the Holy Ghost: and these three are one."

The previous verse is probably the clearest verse in all of the Bible about the trinity.

John 10:30: "I and *my* Father are one."

1 Timothy 3:16: "And without controversy great is the mystery of godliness: God was manifest in the flesh, justified in the Spirit, seen of angels, preached unto the Gentiles, believed on in the world, received up into glory."

It can't be any clearer than the statement 'God was manifest in the flesh'!

John 5:18: "Therefore the Jews sought the more to kill him, because he not only had broken the sabbath, but said also that God was his Father, making himself equal with God."

A teaching that is making the rounds now is that man is so dead in his sins that he cannot repent and believe upon the Lord Jesus Christ for the forgiveness of his sins.

Even the Jews knew that Jesus was claiming to be God, and that is why they tried to stone Him. If they knew 2,000 years ago that Jesus was claiming to be God, don't let the enemy trick you today into thinking He isn't God.

John 11:25, 26: "Jesus said unto her, I am the resurrection, and the life: he that believeth in me, though he were dead, yet shall he live: And whosoever liveth and believeth in me shall never die. Believest thou this?"

Jesus holds the keys to eternal life. He is life and when you believe upon Him, you shall be with Him for all of eternity!

A watchman knows to ask the question, 'Who do you think Jesus is?'

A teaching that is making the rounds now is that man is so dead in his sins that he cannot repent and believe upon the

Why would God ask us to reason with Him, if we were so dead in our sins that we couldn't reason with Him?

Lord Jesus Christ for the forgiveness of his sins.

It is true that man is separated from God by his sins, but that in no way means that he cannot repent and believe. "Throughout the whole Bible, God is presenting principles of truth before sinful, fallen men and imploring them to choose life in Christ rather than death, which is the result of rejecting truth."[56]

Isaiah 1:18: "Come now, and let us reason together, saith the LORD: though your sins be as scarlet, they shall be as white as snow; though they be red like crimson, they shall be as wool."

Why would God ask us to reason with Him, if we were so dead in our sins that we couldn't reason with Him?

Psalm 14:1-3: "The fool hath said in his heart, *There is* no God. They are corrupt, they have done abominable works, *there is* none that doeth good. The LORD looked down from heaven upon the children of men, to see if there were any that did understand, *and* seek God. They are all gone aside, they are *all* together become filthy: *there is* none that doeth good, no, not one."

Remember, the Bible says it is the fool that has said in his heart that there is no God. It is a choice to come to that conclusion. It wasn't that he couldn't come to the conclusion that there is a God, but he wouldn't choose to make that decision; and because of that, there is no good thing in him.

Men are required to make a choice for God in this lifetime. That is why we are here. Period.

Isaiah 55:3: "Incline your ear, and come unto me: hear, and your soul shall live; and I will make an everlasting covenant with you, *even* the sure mercies of David."

Isaiah 55:7: "Let the wicked forsake his way, and the unrighteous man his thoughts: and let him return unto the LORD, and he will have mercy upon him; and to our God, for he will abundantly pardon."

You see, the wicked do have the ability to turn from their sinful ways. As a matter of fact, they are required to do so by God.

How can God judge people that had no ability to repent and believe in Him? It is preposterous to think that.

Genesis 18:25: "… Shall not the Judge of all the earth do right?"

Romans 9:14: "What shall we say then? *Is there* unrighteousness with God? God forbid."

1 John 4:7 says, "Beloved, let us love one another: for love is of God; and every one that loveth is born of God, and knoweth God."

God is a loving being. You cannot separate love from who God is.

The loving God of the Bible does not want people to perish, but have everlasting life! That is why He created them with the ability, and not inability, to choose.

2 Peter 3:9: "The Lord is not slack concerning his promise, as some men count slackness; but is longsuffering to us-ward, not willing that any should perish, but that all should come to repentance."

The loving God of the Bible does not want people to perish, but have everlasting life! That is why He created them with the ability, and not inability, to choose. There is not one verse in the Bible that says man cannot believe upon the gospel of Jesus Christ.

John 3:19, 20: "And this is the condemnation, that light is come into the world, and men loved darkness rather than light, because their deeds were evil. For every one that doeth evil hateth the light, neither cometh to the light, lest his deeds should be reproved."

It is not Biblically accurate to say that people cannot repent and believe upon the Lord Jesus Christ for the forgiveness of their sins. People can and do make that choice.

Men loved the darkness and not the light. It doesn't mean they couldn't repent and go towards the light. But they loved the darkness. It had their affections and God did not.

Matthew 4:17: "From that time Jesus began to preach, and to say, Repent: for the kingdom of heaven is at hand."

Who was Jesus talking to here? He was talking with everyone in front of him. Why? Because everyone has the ability to repent: The only question is will they do it?

As you can see, it is not Biblically accurate to say that people cannot repent and believe upon the Lord Jesus Christ for the forgiveness of their sins. People can and do make that choice.

One of the more interesting teachings over the centuries that is once again gaining a foothold among Christians is that God has unconditionally elected certain people to go to heaven, because He preselects them for salvation. It has nothing to do with their personal decision. God has decided in eternity past to regenerate certain people who are dead in their sins and aren't seeking Him, and then makes them born again, before they repent and believe. But in order to hold that position, you have to hold to the fact that God has also unconditionally rejected certain people to go to hell, and there is nothing they can do about it. Does that sound like the loving God that we read about in the Bible?

So what is the big problem with that belief? It's simple: How can God hold me accountable for things I didn't do, but rather that He orchestrated to happen in my life?

Acts 10:34: "Then Peter opened *his* mouth, and said, Of a truth I perceive that God is no respecter of persons:"

Acts 10:43: "To him give all the prophets witness, that through his name whosoever believeth in him shall receive remission of sins."

If election is true, God is a respecter of persons. But according to those Scriptures, He clearly is not. God respects faith from the heart. Never forget that whosoever believes in Him shall receive remission of sins. Praise the Lord!

Romans 10:9-11: "That if thou shalt confess with thy mouth the Lord Jesus, and shalt believe in thine heart that God hath raised him from the dead, thou shalt be saved. For with the heart man believeth unto righteousness; and with the mouth confession is made unto salvation. For the scripture saith, Whosoever believeth on him shall not be ashamed."

'Elect' is just another name for a believer. God knew who was going to be saved, because He is all knowing. It is really that simple. God did not preselect who goes to heaven and preselect who goes to hell.

The Bible teaches that election depends on one's belief. When you believe, you are one of the elect.

1 Peter 1:1, 2: "Peter, an apostle of Jesus Christ, to the strangers scattered throughout Pontus, Galatia, Cappadocia, Asia, and Bithynia, Elect according to the foreknowledge of God the Father, through sanctification of the Spirit, unto obedience and sprinkling of the blood of Jesus Christ: Grace unto you, and peace, be multiplied."

'Elect' is just another name for a believer. God knew who was going to be saved, because He is all knowing. It is really that simple. God did not preselect who goes to heaven and preselect who goes to hell. It is totally against His character, and His character matters! You cannot divorce the character of God from the teachings of God. They go hand in hand.

> **1 Timothy 2:4:** "Who will have all men to be saved, and to come unto the knowledge of the truth."

In Dave Hunt's DVD entitled *What Love Is This?*[57], he makes a very interesting observation. He says that in order for this false doctrine of the predestination of the elect to be true, people would have to change the meaning of words in certain verses to fit their theology. For example:

- 'World' must be changed to 'Elect' .... 20 times
- 'Whoever' must be changed to 'Elect' .... 16 times
- 'Whosoever' must be changed to 'Elect' .... 16 times
- 'All' must be changed to 'Elect' .... 16 times
- 'Everyman' must be changed to 'Elect' .... 6 times

Over seventy times, people must change the meaning of certain words in the Scripture to fit their doctrine. None of us have the right to destroy Scripture this way. Changing the meaning of words to fit your doctrine is orchestrated by the devil, not God.

> **Romans 10:12, 13:** "For there is no difference between the Jew and the Greek: for the same Lord over all is rich unto all that call upon him. For whosoever shall call upon the name of the Lord shall be saved."

> **Romans 9:30-33:** "What shall we say then? That the Gentiles, which followed not after righteousness, have attained to righteousness, even the righteousness which is of faith. But Israel, which followed after the law of righteousness, hath not attained to the law of righteousness. Wherefore? Because *they sought it* not by faith, but as it were by the works of the law. For they stumbled at that stumblingstone; As it is written, Behold, I lay in Sion a stumblingstone and rock of offence: and whosoever believeth on him shall not be ashamed."

'Whosoever' means 'whosoever'. It is really that simple. Let the Bible determine what you believe, don't let what you believe determine what you think the Bible says! I firmly believe that many people read the Bible with a preconceived notion of what they think it says or what they want it to say. Take your transparencies off of the Bible as you read it. Let the Bible interpret the Bible, and you will be just fine.

Another false teaching out there that goes hand in hand with the false teaching of election is that Jesus only died for the sins of the elect and not for the sins of the whole world. This concept is called 'limited atonement.' So what do watchmen do? They always go to God's Word for their answers!

> **1 John 2:2:** states, "And he is the propitiation for our sins: and not for ours only, but also for *the sins of* the whole world."

> **John 1:29** says, "The next day John seeth Jesus coming unto him, and saith, Behold the Lamb of God, which taketh away the sin of the world."

> **Isaiah 53:6:** "All we like sheep have gone astray; we have turned every one to his own way; and the LORD hath laid on him the iniquity of us all."

Can you imagine watchmen having to preach, "Ladies & gentlemen we are here to tell you the good news that Jesus died, but only for some of you!"? That is totally absurd!

As one man said about this verse, make sure you go in at the first 'all' and come out at the second 'all,' and you will be just fine! Jesus died on the cross for your sins. Now the question is what will you do about it?

Can you imagine watchmen having to preach, "Ladies & gentlemen we are here to tell you the good news that Jesus died, but only for some of you!"? That is totally absurd! But that is what you would have to preach if you didn't believe that Jesus died for every single sin of every single person.

Another false teaching that exists is that people cannot resist God. Once He has decided to come upon you and make you saved, even if you don't want to believe in Him, there is nothing you can do about it. But in the great account of Stephen in Acts 7, people do have the ability to resist God. Verse 51 says, "Ye stiffnecked and uncircumcised in heart and ears, ye do always resist the Holy Ghost: as your fathers did, so do ye." Yes, you can resist the Holy Ghost. People do it all the time. **The question is when will you surrender to the Holy Ghost?**

> **Galatians 3:1:** "O foolish Galatians, who hath bewitched you, that ye should not obey the truth, before whose eyes Jesus Christ hath been evidently set forth, crucified among you?"

A watchman has to be on guard against all of these false teachings that Satan is throwing at us as we head towards eternity.

> **Colossians 2:8:** "Beware lest any man spoil you through philosophy and vain deceit, after the tradition of men, after the rudiments of the world, and not after Christ."

Men like to create their own ideas. I hear them all the time. It feeds their pride. But the truth of the matter is that there is nothing new under the sun. All these 'new' ideas are actually old ideas from the same enemy. Satan loves to feed Christians anything that will attack the Word of God, and he doesn't care how foolish it sounds or how unscriptural it is.

> **Romans 1:18-20:** "For the wrath of God is revealed from heaven against all ungodliness and unrighteousness of men, who hold the truth in unrighteousness; Because that which may be known of God is manifest in them; for God hath shewed it unto them. For the invisible things of him from the creation of the world are clearly seen, being understood by the things that are made, *even* his eternal power and Godhead; so that they are without excuse:"

If men had no chance at all to repent and believe because in eternity past, God unconditionally rejected them to hell, then they would have this as their excuse before God. But as you can see in Romans 1, because of God's marvelous creation, men will have no excuse on Judgment Day for why they did not find out Who it was that made this grand universe.

There are fables being taught and false prophets preaching everywhere in our world. Are you sure you haven't been deceived by one of them?

And also, why would this all loving God (1 John 4:7; John 3:16) hold back that grace from so many people? What kind of love is that?

There are fables being taught and false prophets preaching everywhere in our world. Are you sure you haven't been deceived by one of them?

> **Deuteronomy 30:19:** "I call heaven and earth to record this day against you, *that* I have set before you life and death, blessing and cursing: therefore choose life, *that* both thou and thy seed may live:"

One of the challenges I give to people all the time is to read their Bibles front to back. Actually it is a good thing to do every year. It is impossible to read your Bible front to back and not realize that every one of us has to make decisions. We have to make choices, and we are responsible for those choices. We have the ability and responsibility to choose God or not choose God.

The issue of these false teachings is a serious one, because it concerns the character of God, the Gospel, and who God is (or isn't). This is not a secondary issue, but a primary one. People keep telling me that this is a side issue and not a main issue, but anytime you are talking about the character of God

Counterfeit money is actually easy to spot for a bank teller or a casino employee who regularly handles money. It just doesn't feel right when they touch it.

and the gospel, it is a main issue. Period.

Play the concept of election all the way through: You are a parent, and you have four children. God has elected one of them to go to heaven and rejected three of them to go to hell. So every night when you hug and kiss them good night and tuck them in, you have to think in your head, "I wonder which of these four God is sending to hell for eternity." How does that sound to you Mom and Dad? Oh, and by the way, there is nothing you can do about it. So when you train up a child in the way they should go, and you teach them the things of God when they sit down, rise up, walk by the way, and lie down, that has no—and I do mean no—effect on how your kids will turn out. They have already been elected or rejected by God.

We have a saying down South: That dog won't hunt. It means, don't even try it. When you look at election this way, it doesn't pass the smell test, the logic test, the dog won't hunt test, or the Biblical test. Period!

> **Titus 1:9:** "Holding fast the faithful word as he hath been taught, that he may be able by sound doctrine both to exhort and to convince the gainsayers."

'Doctrine' means instruction or teaching. We must have sound doctrine as watchmen. Counterfeit money is actually easy to spot for a bank teller or a casino employee who regularly handles money. It just doesn't feel right when they touch it. And one thing money handlers must never do is play with the counterfeit money, because if their fingers get desensitized to it, then they may not be able to tell the difference between it and the real thing down the road. Remember to study your Bibles watchmen, so it is easier to spot the false doctrines in the days ahead.

2 John 9: "Whosoever transgresseth, and abideth not in the doctrine of Christ, hath not God. He that abideth in the doctrine of Christ, he hath both the Father and the Son."

God takes doctrine very seriously. Do you?

Ephesians 4:14, 15: "That we *henceforth* be no more children, tossed to and fro, and carried about with every wind of doctrine, by the sleight of men, *and* cunning craftiness, whereby they lie in wait to deceive; But speaking the truth in love, may grow up into him in all things, which is the head, *even* Christ:"

Watchmen know what they believe and won't allow themselves to be carried away by false teachings.

Matthew 22:29: "Jesus answered and said unto them, Ye do err, not knowing the scriptures, nor the power of God."

Watchmen are very careful to know the Scriptures. We cannot lead people astray in these last days. We must sound the trumpet loudly, but also clearly.

Deuteronomy 13:1-5: "If there arise among you a prophet, or a dreamer of dreams, and giveth thee a sign or a wonder, And the sign or the wonder come to pass, whereof he spake unto thee, saying, Let us go after other gods, which thou hast not known, and let us serve them; Thou shalt not hearken unto the words of that prophet, or that dreamer of dreams: for the LORD your God proveth you, to know whether ye love the LORD your God with all your heart and with all your soul. Ye shall walk after the LORD your God, and fear him, and keep his commandments, and obey his voice, and ye shall serve him, and cleave unto him. And that prophet, or that dreamer of dreams, shall be put to death; because he hath spoken to turn *you* away from the LORD your God, which brought you out of the land of Egypt, and redeemed you out of the house of bondage, to thrust thee out of the way which the LORD

thy God commanded thee to walk in. So shalt thou put the evil away from the midst of thee."

The Bible is not a buffet from which we can pick and choose what we want to believe or what fits our thinking.

If the miracle worker doesn't point you to the God of the Bible, get as far away from that person as you can.

John 8:31, 32: "Then said Jesus to those Jews which believed on him, If ye continue in my word, *then* are ye my disciples indeed; And ye shall know the truth, and the truth shall make you free."

Once a watchman knows Biblical truth, we are free and free indeed!

Be on guard watchmen: A church is supposed to be where we get trained up. We need good, challenging, Biblical messages in the coming days. Be very careful about these seeker churches that won't preach sin, repentance, hell, the holiness of God, and God's judgment. This is not the time to water down any message. It is not time for our churches to be 'relevant' as I keep hearing from people. Our job is to be Biblical and nothing less.

Jeremiah 23:29: "*Is* not my word like as a fire? saith the LORD; and like a hammer *that* breaketh the rock in pieces?"

Never forget, watchmen, how powerful the words of God are all the days of your life.

"If you have a Bible that's falling apart, you'll have a life that's not."[58]
—ADRIAN ROGERS

The Bible is not a buffet from which we can pick and choose what we want to believe or what fits our thinking. Taking only bits and pieces of the Word is the same as taking only what we want from Jesus, since He is the Word. Some people like the salvation and the unconditional love they receive from Him, but they don't like the obedience and the dying to self part of a relationship with Him. *Never forget that the Bible is a feast that needs to be enjoyed!*

There are many tests in life as a watchman. False doctrines will pop up to see if you are going to follow the crowd or follow the teachings of God's Word. When you make your stand, it might cost you something. But a watchman already knows deep within his heart that our Lord is worth the persecution. A watchman knows to even be careful of miracles. Satan is on the prowl seeking to get you off the narrow road in the final days. Stand upon the truths of God's Word, and make sure in the coming days that you are an immovable force that God can use to proclaim His truths anywhere He decides to place you!

…the Bible is a feast that needs to be enjoyed!

Think about one of your friends who has died without the Lord. Listen for a second. Can you hear them? Can you hear them begging and screaming in hell: "Please go and talk to my relatives about Jesus." Wrestle with that for a second.

Chapter 9
No Crossing Over

"Consider that all these torments of body and soul are without intermission. Be their suffering ever so extreme, be their pain ever so intense, there is no possibility of their fainting away, no, not for one moment ... They are all eye, all ear, all sense. Every instant of their duration it may be said of their whole frame that they are 'Trembling alive all o'er, and smart and agonize at every pore.' And of this duration there is no end ... Neither the pain of the body nor of soul is any nearer an end than it was millions of ages ago."[59]
–JOHN WESLEY

Luke 16:19-31:
V. 19: "There was a certain rich man, which was clothed in purple and fine linen, and fared sumptuously every day:"

Think about how you receive the blessings of God. Do we use them for ourselves, or do we use them for others? Do we ever think about the fact that we may fall off of our pedestal one day, and that we might need someone to reach out and help us? Are you treating others the way you would want to be treated if you were in their spot? If not, today is a new day to start doing just that.

Deuteronomy 8:17, 18: "And thou say in thine heart, My power and the might of *mine* hand hath gotten me this wealth. But thou shalt remember the LORD thy God: for *it is* he that giveth thee power to get wealth, that he may establish his covenant which he sware unto thy fathers, as *it is* this day."

Never forget it is God who gives us wealth. He is the One who blesses. We need to be thankful and grateful for all of the blessings that we have.

So do you want to be highly regarded by men or highly regarded by God? Many times when you have wealth, you can show off all of your toys, but will any of those toys matter the day that you die?

> **V. 20** "And there was a certain beggar named Lazarus, which was laid at his gate, full of sores,"

At this point, we now know that this isn't just some story, but a true account. Jesus never calls people by their real names in any of His parables. Both Lazarus and Abraham are mentioned here. This is a very real account of very real people on the other side.

So what do you do when you see a homeless person? Do you avoid them? Walk the other way? Have you already decided they are going to rob you, so you get out of harm's way?

I was leaving a festival once after a long day of witnessing, and there was a guy sitting on a brick wall as I was heading to my car. He said, "Sir can you help me, I have no money." I was really tired on this hot summer day, so it was nice to stop and chat. As we talked, he let me know that he had just gotten out of prison. We had a nice talk about Jesus. He had done some reading about Him while he was in jail. I decided to financially bless him. He sat there with tears in his eyes like I had given him a million dollars! It was so interesting. He then told me that I was the first person he had asked all day for money. He was too ashamed. The prison system bought him a bus ticket, and he got dropped off in Atlanta. It was beneath him to beg, but he finally reached that point of desperation. I was so glad that God chose me to be the guy walking past him at that time. I really hope that I made God look good in that moment.

One of the bolder guys on the streets of Atlanta is John. John is homeless, and he tells me that he likes that lifestyle. Whenever we are at events downtown, John always seems to walk by. He always comes over and helps me pass out tracts. He opens up his mouth to share the gospel as well. He knows his Scriptures very well. I make sure that I bless John to help with some of his needs. John has done more witnessing than so many folks who own a home. I can't wait to see his treasures in heaven one day!

> **V. 21** "And desiring to be fed with the crumbs which fell from the rich man's table: moreover the dogs came and licked his sores."

Life goes by so quickly, and you don't get a do over. You don't get a mulligan. You don't get a second chance at this crazy place called earth. One shot, and then Judgment Day.

Sometimes, you get so hungry that you will take anything. Even the crumbs from someone's table will look like a five course meal. One thing I often pray before I eat is not to take that food before me for granted. Because in an instant, God could take it all away, and I would be looking for someone's crumbs.

> **V. 22** "And it came to pass, that the beggar died, and was carried by the angels into Abraham's bosom: the rich man also died, and was buried;"

Rich or poor, we are all going to the grave. Go visit a cemetery sometime, and look around. It is very interesting to see young people in there and old people. But whether you live 15 years or 115 years, compared to eternity, it all goes by so fast. At a church where I was speaking recently, there were a lot of white-haired folks. I love white-haired people! They are usually so gracious and kind, and they are always full of wisdom. I was trying to make a point to the younger people, so I asked the older people, "Did life go by pretty quickly?" You should have seen all of these handsome and pretty wrinkly faces nodding their heads up and down! Life goes by so quickly, and you don't get a do over. You don't get a mulligan. You don't get a second chance at this crazy place called earth. One shot, and then Judgment Day. So how are you living this one chance on the merry-go-round of life?

V. 23 "And in hell he lift up his eyes, being in torments, and seeth Abraham afar off, and Lazarus in his bosom."

Hell is a very real place. Don't buy into this notion of hell being some place that is a party, where people will be hanging out with their friends, or a place with 'a bunch of really good bands' as one person told me.

The rich man is conscious. His eyes work just fine, and he doesn't like what he sees. Some people believe death means life is over and that there is nothing on the other side, but as you can see, this man is very much alive. Death just unlocked the door to the other side for the rich man, and he does not like what is behind that door. His own choices have brought him to this point.

Hell is a very real place. Don't buy into this notion of hell being some place that is a party, where people will be hanging out with their friends, or a place with 'a bunch of really good bands' as one person told me. Those are all lies by the enemy to get people not to take their rejection of Jesus seriously. Watchmen must always take hell seriously. They must pull out the trumpet and warn people that not only is trouble coming in this life for being disobedient to God, but trouble is rushing towards them in an eternal sense as well.

Robert Ingersoll, one of America's famous atheists, said, "The idea of Hell was born of revenge and brutality on the one side, and cowardice on the other. I have no respect for any man who preaches it! I dislike the doctrine, I hate it, I despise it, I defy this doctrine."[60]

One thing I always tell people is that it doesn't matter what you believe, it only matters what is true. Even if you do not believe in hell, it is a real place. The Scriptures cannot be any clearer on this subject.

Don't forget that it is Jesus speaking in this passage. If there is no hell, then Jesus is a liar who has deceived billions of people about eternity. But we know that does not fit His character at all.

Polycarp, the disciple of John, knew how real hell was. When he was threatened with death for his beliefs, his response was: "Thou threatenest me with fire which burneth for an hour, and after a little is extinguished, but art ignorant of the fire of the coming judgment and of eternal punishment, reserved for the ungodly. But why tarriest thou? Bring forth what thou wilt."[61]

Polycarp knew hell was real and eternal, and he wanted to warn people about going there.

Hell is described in the Bible as 'a place of unquenchable fire, punishment, misery, and pain where your memory works and you have remorse,' a place of 'thirst, frustration, and anger,' and 'the wrath of God.'

The Scriptures also list who will be in hell: Satan, the Antichrist, the false prophet, fallen angels, Judas Iscariot, and all unsaved people.

Revelation 21:8: "But the fearful, and unbelieving, and the abominable, and murderers, and whoremongers, and sorcerers, and idolaters, and all liars, shall have their part in the lake which burneth with fire and brimstone: which is the second death."

God made it simple and even listed the people who would go there. As little as telling one lie will send you there. God is holy and God is pure. Every sin is nasty to Him. Thankfully the blood of Jesus Christ cleanses us from all sin or we would all be in an eternal world of hurt.

2 Thessalonians 1:9: "Who shall be punished with everlasting destruction from the presence of the Lord, and from the glory of his power;"

Hell is a place of torments. It is a place where people do feel pain. As you can see here, the rich man's eyes are working, and so are his other senses.

Revelation 14:10, 11: "The same shall drink of the wine of the wrath of God, which is poured out without mixture into the cup of his indignation; and he shall be tormented with fire and brimstone in the presence of the holy angels, and in the presence of the Lamb: And the smoke of their torment ascendeth up for ever and ever: and they have no rest day nor night, who worship the beast and his image, and whosoever receiveth the mark of his name."

Revelation 20:10-15: "And the devil that deceived them was cast into the lake of fire and brimstone, where the beast and the false prophet *are*, and shall be tormented day and night for ever and ever. And I saw a great white throne, and him that sat on it, from whose face the earth and the heaven fled away; and there was found no place for them. And I saw the dead, small and great, stand before God; and the books were opened: and another book was opened, which is *the book* of life: and the dead were judged out of those things which were written in the books, according to their works. And the sea gave up the dead which were in it; and death and hell delivered up the dead which were in them: and they were judged every man according to their works. And death and hell were cast into the lake of fire. This is the second death. And whosoever was not found written in the book of life was cast into the lake of fire."

Hell is a place of torments. It is a place where people do feel pain. As you can see here, the rich man's eyes are working, and so are his other senses.

"This passage is very clear; this is a real man in a real place, experiencing real torment. This is a literal man in a literal body in a literal place called Hell!"[62]

V. 24 "And he cried and said, Father Abraham, have mercy on me, and send Lazarus, that he may dip the tip of his finger in water, and cool my tongue; for I am tormented in this flame."

The rich man is crying out; he is speaking loudly, because he needs help. What does he want? Mercy. Do you know what everyone wants? Mercy! I want mercy; I don't want to get what I deserve. I want to get what I don't deserve. I don't deserve favor in this life, but God graciously grants it to me. And I definitely want mercy in the next life, as well. And that can only be provided by the blood of Jesus Christ, and the decision I make for Him while I'm on planet earth.

Psalm 136:1: "O give thanks unto the LORD; for *he is* good: for his mercy *endureth* for ever."

Psalm 86:5 "For thou, Lord, *art* good, and ready to forgive; and plenteous in mercy unto all them that call upon thee."

God is a wonderfully merciful God. He doesn't want anyone to go anywhere near hell. Do you have the mercy of God? Make sure you realize, there is a time for people when God's mercy is shut off. They no longer have access to it. Their rejection of God is complete, and they can no longer receive His forgiveness or the mercy that He wanted to shower upon them.

The flames of hell are real. Have you ever experienced one of those long, hot summer days where all you wanted was some cool water to quench your thirst? We used to play basketball at this elementary school when I was younger, and we would gather on these hot Sunday afternoons, wearing our Chuck Taylors, and run up and down that tar basketball court for hours. We would bring a huge cooler of iced down Cokes and Gatorade. Do you know people in hell would crawl all the way across the lake of fire just for one sip of those Gatorades? But there is no chance of that ever happening. Their fate is sealed. All hope is gone for them. Their rejection of Jesus is complete.

V. 25 "But Abraham said, Son, remember that thou in thy lifetime receivedst thy good things, and likewise Lazarus evil things: but now he is comforted, and thou art tormented."

The rich man consciously remembers the details of his life. He remembers Lazarus at the gate. He remembers that he did nothing for Lazarus when he had the chance.

So what would you trade? Would you trade a penthouse in New York City or a beachside mansion in Palm Beach for eternity with God in heaven? Don't be fooled though: People can worship a two-bedroom house as much as a mansion, and a Kia as much as a Lamborghini. It is really a heart issue. What are you really worshipping? Watchmen always know Who they are worshipping and Who belongs first and foremost in their lives!

People can worship a two-bedroom house as much as a mansion, and a Kia as much as a Lamborghini. It is really a heart issue.

V. 26 "And beside all this, between us and you there is a great gulf fixed: so that they which would pass from hence to you cannot; neither can they pass to us, that *would come* from thence."

And if all that wasn't enough, you cannot cross from one side to the other. When you die, judgment is set. There is no second chance to get right with Jesus Christ.

Hebrews 9:27: "And as it is appointed unto men once to die, but after this the judgment:"

Think about that. People in hell would want to get out and go be with people in heaven. People in heaven would want to go get those people out of hell. But there is no crossing over. Watchmen know that they must do their job while they are still alive. We don't warn people about their impending judgment after they die, we warn them before they die.

V. 27 "Then he said, I pray thee therefore, father, that thou wouldest send him to my father's house:"

Why in the world would someone beg God for someone to go to his father's house? Because when people die, their conscience still works.

Why in the world would someone beg God for someone to go to his father's house? Because when people die, their conscience still works. They will think about the things they did in their life that caused them to go to hell. They will think about their rejection of Jesus Christ that sealed their eternal fate. But something interesting is happening here. You can see that the rich man has become a very concerned man. He may not have been concerned about the things of God when he was living on earth, but that has all changed now.

V. 28 "For I have five brethren; that he may testify unto them, lest they also come into this place of torment."

Wait a minute. This rich man in hell wants someone to testify to his brothers? We don't even know his relationship with his brothers. They may have been friends, but they may not. He may have shared his wealth with them, but he may not have. Why does he care about his brothers? Because your feelings don't shut off when you die. They continue for all of eternity. What does he want testified to his brothers? It is easy to figure out: He doesn't want them to come to this place of torment. They need Jesus! He wants someone to go and tell his relatives about Jesus Christ. The rich man knows God has not preselected his relatives to go to heaven or hell. They have to

make a choice. They need the right information about Jesus, and they need it now.

Isn't it interesting that people in heaven believe in personal evangelism? We know that, because we see people in the Bible doing it all the time. And now you have just witnessed a man in hell who believes in personal evangelism. He is begging for someone to go talk with his brothers. Yet how many times do I meet people that say they are Christians, but they do not share their faith in Jesus Christ, and therefore must not believe in personal evangelism. Watchmen let that never be. We are compelled to warn the lost. That is our calling.

Think about one of your friends who has died without the Lord. Listen for a second. Can you hear them?

Think about one of your friends who has died without the Lord. Listen for a second. Can you hear them? Can you hear them begging and screaming in hell: 'Please go and talk to my relatives about Jesus so they don't come to this place of torment!"? Wrestle with that for a second. Picture that person there and then try and hear the words. They are not making this statement with no emotion. This is serious eternal business. They now know the importance of knowing Jesus Christ, but it is too late for them. And they do not want anyone else to come to this place of torment.

Take some time and picture any lost person in hell, whether it is a celebrity like Frank Sinatra or Steve Jobs who we know rejected Jesus Christ, or maybe the person you once saw at the gas station or mall. Picture them. Listen to their voices. They are screaming in torment and agony. They do not want anyone else to go to that place of torment. Do you have the same desire as they do for people not to die without the Lord? Watchmen always have that type of focus. Their minds are steeled in doing the things of God. They are focused, and there is no turning back for the Biblical watchman.

V. 29 "Abraham saith unto him, They have Moses and the prophets; let them hear them."

Abraham is very clear here. These folks already have the Bible. They have the writings of Moses called the Torah. They have all the answers right in front of them. They have all of the prophecies in the Bible that they can believe in and find truth.

John 6:45: "It is written in the prophets, And they shall be all taught of God. Every man therefore that hath heard, and hath learned of the Father, cometh unto me."

But the real question is will they seek?

Deuteronomy 4:29: "But if from thence thou shalt seek the LORD thy God, thou shalt find *him*, if thou seek him with all thy heart and with all thy soul."

Hebrews 11:6: "But without faith it is impossible to please *him*: for he that cometh to God must believe that he is, and *that* he is a rewarder of them that diligently seek him."

Remind people that they have the responsibility to seek and find out who God is. They can seek the things of the world, or seek the things of God. It is their choice.

V. 30 "And he said, Nay, father Abraham: but if one went unto them from the dead, they will repent."

Really? Is it true that if these men saw someone who was dead that they would repent and believe? I would have to say no, because Jesus died on the cross and rose from the dead. The eyewitness testimony of His resurrection is incontrovertible. You literally have to deny facts not to believe in Jesus and His resurrection. What it really comes down to is our desires and our wants. People don't want to believe in God, and they don't want to believe in Jesus. And what is the main reason for that? They don't want to admit that they are not in control. Once there is a God, it means I am not in control. But if you reject Jesus so you can think you are in control, it will only be for a short time. Once you die, you will know for sure that it is God who sits on the throne and not you.

> **V. 31** "And he said unto him, If they hear not Moses and the prophets, neither will they be persuaded, though one rose from the dead."

As you can tell, these brothers didn't want to listen. They didn't want to listen to truth, and they would reject it even if someone came out of the grave and told them. It is their pride getting in the way. Their pride says, "I am the man." But as usual, reality is different than the fiction we are living in.

> **Psalm 10:4:** "The wicked, through the pride of his countenance, will not seek *after God*: God is not in all his thoughts."

> **Proverbs 16:18:** "Pride *goeth* before destruction, and an haughty spirit before a fall."

If the rich man could come back to planet earth for five seconds, he would repent of his sins and become born again. But he does not have that opportunity.

Yes, an all loving God will allow people to go to hell. He will allow people to follow their choices right into eternity. Why?

> **Deuteronomy 32:3-5:** "Because I will publish the name of the LORD: ascribe ye greatness unto our God. *He is* the Rock, his work *is* perfect: for all his ways are judgment: a God of truth and without iniquity, just and right is he. They have corrupted themselves, their spot *is* not *the spot* of his children: *they are* a perverse and crooked generation."

He is a just God. And because of His justness, people will be punished for their sins.

> **Proverbs 16:25:** "There is a way that seemeth right unto a man, but the end thereof *are* the ways of death."

He will not force someone to love and obey Him. He will allow people to follow their unbelief all the way into eternity.

Matthew 25:41: "Then shall he say also unto them on the left hand, Depart from me, ye cursed, into everlasting fire, prepared for the devil and his angels:"

Hell was made for the devil and his angels, but people have the right to go there if they want to. I had a guy tell me that God wouldn't send him to hell. I actually agreed with him! He couldn't believe I agreed with his position. I then said, "All God will do is put His stamp of approval on your decision to reject Him and Jesus." People truly send themselves to hell when you think about it. God has provided the way to Him through Jesus, but you must either accept or reject Him.

"Heaven is real, hell is hot, and eternity is long."…A watchman knows it is time to speak up. A watchman knows this isn't a game.

But a watchman will always want to do something about people going the wrong way for eternity.

As one person said, "Heaven is real, hell is hot, and eternity is long." A watchman knows all three of these facts. A watchman knows it is time to speak up. A watchman knows this isn't a game. Please hear me, watchmen. This is very serious. We do not want to see anyone take his or her last breath without Jesus and go to hell for all of eternity. Watchmen know people may ridicule them for talking about hell, but watchmen don't care. Watchmen know sounding the trumpet and warning people about hell is more important than any words that can be hurled back in their direction.

Are you prepared to meet
thy God, and have you
prepared others for
that day?

Chapter 10
Time No More

"We ought to be living as if Jesus died yesterday, rose this morning,
and is coming back this afternoon."[63]
–ADRIAN ROGERS

Romans 13:11, 12: "And that, knowing the time, that now *it is* high
time to awake out of sleep: for now *is* our salvation nearer than when
we believed. The night is far spent, the day is at hand: let us therefore
cast off the works of darkness, and let us put on the armour of light."

A watchman must always know the time. He or she must
know how late the hour is. The days are running short.
For that person who just took his or her last breath today, there
is no second chance. A watchman cannot allow the affairs of
this world to take precedence in their life.

2 Timothy 2:1-4: "Thou therefore, my son, be strong in the grace that
is in Christ Jesus. And the things that thou hast heard of me among
many witnesses, the same commit thou to faithful men, who shall be
able to teach others also. Thou therefore endure hardness, as a good
soldier of Jesus Christ. No man that warreth entangleth himself with
the affairs of *this* life; that he may please him who hath chosen him
to be a soldier."

The things of this world cannot grasp a watchman. We
know they have no significance in the light of eternity. God's
words cannot be any more clear.

James 4:4: "Ye adulterers and adulteresses, know ye not that the
friendship of the world is enmity with God? whosoever therefore
will be a friend of the world is the enemy of God."

1 John 2:15-17: "Love not the world, neither the things *that are* in
the world. If any man love the world, the love of the Father is not in
him. For all that *is* in the world, the lust of the flesh, and the lust of

Do not be a friend of this world that is passing away. If something does not have eternal value, it will end up being a waste of your time.

the eyes, and the pride of life, is not of the Father, but is of the world. And the world passeth away, and the lust thereof: but he that doeth the will of God abideth for ever."

Do not be a friend of this world that is passing away. If something does not have eternal value, it will end up being a waste of your time. Because the night is far spent and the day is at hand, you must stay focused on the task at hand.

Daniel 9:9-14: "To the Lord our God *belong* mercies and forgivenesses, though we have rebelled against him; Neither have we obeyed the voice of the LORD our God, to walk in his laws, which he set before us by his servants the prophets. Yea, all Israel have transgressed thy law, even by departing, that they might not obey thy voice; therefore the curse is poured upon us, and the oath that *is* written in the law of Moses the servant of God, because we have sinned against him. And he hath confirmed his words, which he spake against us, and against our judges that judged us, by bringing upon us a great evil: for under the whole heaven hath not been done as hath been done upon Jerusalem. As *it is* written in the law of Moses, all this evil is come upon us: yet made we not our prayer before the LORD our God, that we might turn from our iniquities, and understand thy truth. Therefore hath the LORD watched upon the evil, and brought it upon us: for the LORD our God *is* righteous in all his works which he doeth: for we obeyed not his voice."

God is a merciful and loving God who gives us time to repent, but He does finally reach a point with people and nations when He says enough is enough. Your time is up.

Romans 2:4: "Or despisest thou the riches of his goodness and forbearance and longsuffering; not knowing that the goodness of God leadeth thee to repentance?"

It is His goodness that wants us to return to Him. It is His goodness that allows wicked, evil sinners to still be alive this day. He is giving them time to repent, because He is so kind and merciful. But the real question is: Who is warning them of their impending judgment? We must warn people and nations of the consequences if they do not repent. This is such a wicked and depraved world. Sin is running rampant everywhere. People are made in the image of God, and it seems like no one cares. We will treat animals better than we do people. That can never be named amongst the watchmen. We know every soul matters to God. We warn, because we love. God is going to bring massive judgment on this world, because of its wickedness. We must make sure people are prepared.

It is His goodness that wants us to return to Him. It is His goodness that allows wicked, evil sinners to still be alive this day. He is giving them time to repent, because He is so kind and merciful.

If there are only two minutes left in a basketball game, and you are down eight points, what do you do? You pick up the pace. You press, you intentionally foul to slow the clock down, and you shoot three pointers. Time is running very, very short here on planet earth for so many souls. Watchmen, pick the pace up while we still have time!

James 4:14: "Whereas ye know not what *shall be* on the morrow. For what *is* your life? It is even a vapour, that appeareth for a little time, and then vanisheth away."

Death can show up quickly for any one of us. Death shows up on each one of our day planners at some point. Are you prepared to meet thy God, and have you prepared others for that day?

I sat next to a military helicopter pilot once on a flight to Florida, and we began to talk. He was just coming home permanently from Afghanistan, and he couldn't wait to see his family. So, I asked him if he had any close calls flying helicopters. He told me that on a training mission in Vietnam, one of the bolts of his helicopter broke and shot straight up through one of the blades. The chopper started going down, but he got everybody ready for the crash landing, and everyone got out safely. But then he said, "It was amazing to see how quick-

ly a helicopter could burn to the ground." He said that when the fire had burned out, all that was left was the shell of the aircraft. That close to eternity, but God allows Carlos more time to live.

Life goes by so, so quickly. If you knew on Thursday that the tsunami was going to hit the next day, what would you have done?

You could be in Japan with a weekend full of plans, but at 2:45 on a Friday afternoon, the earth might shake. And it might just be a 9.0 earthquake. As a matter of fact, it might cause the water to move, and in just a short amount of time, countless people head off into eternity because of a tsunami. Life goes by so, so quickly. If you knew on Thursday that the tsunami was going to hit the next day, what would you have done? You would have warned many people. The real question is who warned those people about their meeting with their Maker? That is what watchmen do!

In parts of Japan, there are actually stones on the hillside that warn people not to build their homes below a certain line. It is because tsunamis have come through before and destroyed everything below that point. One town had no one die in the 2011 tsunami. Why? They heeded the stones' warning.[64]

If you will heed the warnings here on earth, you need to heed the eternal warnings, as well. Watchmen know it is time to warn everyone about what is awaiting them after their last breath.

When you saw video footage of the tsunami in Japan, you could hear the sirens going off in the background. That is what watchmen do when we blow the trumpet: We warn people–but it will always be their choice what to do with that warning.

If you will heed the warnings here on earth, you need to heed the eternal warnings, as well. Watchmen know it is time to warn everyone about what is awaiting them after their last breath.

Psalm 90:4: "For a thousand years in thy sight *are but* as yesterday when it is past, and *as* a watch in the night."

Psalm 90:12: "So teach *us* to number our days, that we may apply *our* hearts unto wisdom."

A Biblical watchman must be able to number his days. A watchman can't say, "When I get older, I am going to…" No. Today is way too important.

2 Corinthians 6:2: "(…behold, now *is* the day of salvation.)"

Today is the day of salvation for someone. Today is the day to warn someone about eternity. Today is the most precious day you will ever live. Tomorrow is promised to no man. A watchman uses his time wisely.

Who was the first Caesar? Who was the first NFL draft pick last year? Who won the NCAA basketball title five years ago? We need to see our own mortality. Time is scooting by so quickly. Are you sure you are using your time wisely for God's purposes?

What if you put two jars on your countertop, and filled one of them with 3,640 marbles, each one representing one Saturday for the average 70-year lifespan. Now think about taking one marble each week and moving it over to the other jar. You could literally watch your life pass before your eyes! All of the sudden, as your time is moving from one jar to the  next, you can see the importance of not wasting your time on things that will have zero eternal significance when you stand in front of God.

*The people you will see with your eyes today are living eternal beings. **They will be alive worshipping before the throne of God forever and ever, or they will be screaming in the bowels of hell for all of eternity.***

And never forget that each one of us will be dead a whole lot longer than we will ever be alive! The cemetery is a reminder of that. Those old tombstones that wear down over the annals of time show us this truth. But don't forget that all of those people in those graves are still alive to this day and will be alive for all of eternity!

How do you see people? Do you see white, black, Asian, Hispanic, rich, poor, athletic, non-athletic, smart, an average thinker, beautiful, or average looking? The people you will see with your eyes today are living eternal beings. ***They will be alive worshipping before the throne of God forever and ever, or they will be screaming in the bowels of hell for all of eternity.*** So let me ask you one more time: How do you see people today?

I was wrestling with the thief on the cross account in the Bible the other day. I began to wonder if his family was there when he died, or if he had defamed the family name so badly that they didn't even show up for his execution. Were they

there when their son was crucified on that cross? If they weren't, boy did they miss out on a great ending!

Luke 23:42, 43: "And he said unto Jesus, Lord, remember me when thou comest into thy kingdom. And Jesus said unto him, Verily I say unto thee, To day shalt thou be with me in paradise."

Jesus was a watchman all the way until His last breath! He was making sure everyone in front of Him continued to hear the truth about God. And because of that, there is a forgiven thief who knows more about eternity than anyone reading this book! Jesus finished well for His Father, and all watchmen are called to do the same.

Jesus was a watchman all the way until His last breath! He was making sure everyone in front of Him continued to hear the truth about God. And because of that, there is a forgiven thief who knows more about eternity than anyone reading this book!

Hebrews 12:2: "Looking unto Jesus the author and finisher of *our* faith; who for the joy that was set before him endured the cross, despising the shame, and is set down at the right hand of the throne of God."

2 Timothy 4:7: "I have fought a good fight, I have finished *my* course, I have kept the faith:"

I was reading a story about a dad on his deathbed. He said his good-byes and looked straight at two of his boys and told them that he would never see them again, because they were not saved. He let them know that he loved them, but they were lost for eternity without Jesus. Just a short time after his death, both of his sons repented of their sins and became born again! Dad was a watchman all the way until his last breath!

Peter may have denied Jesus three times, but that was not the end of the story! He finished very well for the Lord Jesus Christ. **Watchmen are people who finish well.**

Peter may have denied Jesus three times, but that was not the end of the story! He finished very well for the Lord Jesus Christ. **Watchmen are people who finish well.**

The pastor of a church where I was speaking once told his congregation that he wanted one hundred percent of them sharing their faith in Jesus Christ. It was clear that he wanted all of his flock to be watchmen and to finish well!

As I was walking into my hotel room in Nebraska one evening, I noticed a man coming down the hall. So I took my time opening my door, and as he passed by, we struck up a conversation. As we were talking, he told me that one time he had flown to Ireland to play golf with some buddies. He landed and checked his phone messages only to learn that his sixteen-year-old daughter had been killed in an ATV accident. She had gone off the side of a road and went face first into a rock. He then told me that he got back on the exact same plane to fly home to bury his daughter. You can imagine how much he missed her. He was a Christian man, but was struggling with this whole situation. So I said, "If you could have had her fifteen years or sixteen, which would you have taken?" He responded, "Sixteen." I said, "If you could have had her fourteen years or sixteen years, which would you have taken?" He said, "Sixteen, and I know where you are going with this!" I looked at him and let him know that he would have rather had her twenty years, see her get married and give him grandkids, etc. But none of us are guaranteed tomorrow. Instead of looking at a situation like that as someone dying early, shouldn't we be thankful that we got to be with her for

sixteen wonderful years? We should be thankful for every day we have with our loved ones, and thankful to be alive one more day for Him. If we looked at things that way, we would be much more thankful as we live this life! I can't believe I get another day to live for Him!

> **Psalm 126:6:** "He that goeth forth and weepeth, bearing precious seed, shall doubtless come again with rejoicing, bringing his sheaves *with him*."

> **2 Corinthians 5:10:** "For we must all appear before the judgment seat of Christ; that every one may receive the things *done* in *his* body, according to that he hath done, whether *it be* good or bad."

Are you focusing on what will matter when you die and not wasting time on things that won't? Maybe you should even make a list of the things going on in your life that have no eternal significance.

> **1 Corinthians 3:12, 13:** "Now if any man build upon this foundation gold, silver, precious stones, wood, hay, stubble; Every man's work shall be made manifest: for the day shall declare it, because it shall be revealed by fire; and the fire shall try every man's work of what sort it is."

Watchmen, your works will be judged one day. Are you focusing on what will matter when you die and not wasting time on things that won't? Maybe you should even make a list of the things going on in your life that have no eternal significance. Then, put it to the side, or throw it away if necessary. A Biblical watchman must have a laser beam-like focus.

> **Luke 19:10:** "For the Son of man is come to seek and to save that which was lost."

The Christian law firm that helps me when I run into issues when I'm out witnessing told me about a street preacher that got arrested in San Diego. The district attorney told the police to get him out of jail, because he had done nothing wrong. When they arrived at the jail to let him go, he asked them if he could just have ten more minutes in the cell! What was he doing, watchmen? You got it. He was witnessing to a lost soul that needed Jesus Christ!

Proverbs 28:1: "The wicked flee when no man pursueth: but the righteous are bold as a lion."

Watchmen have to be bold. There is no other choice. But a true watchman doesn't want there to be another option or another choice! One way and one way only for a watchman: Bold!

Ephesians 6:18-20: "Praying always with all prayer and supplication in the Spirit, and watching thereunto with all perseverance and supplication for all saints; And for me, that utterance may be given unto me, that I may open my mouth boldly, to make known the mystery of the gospel, For which I am an ambassador in bonds: that therein I may speak boldly, as I ought to speak."

If one of the all time great watchmen, Paul, had to pray for boldness, so do we. We must be endued with power by the Holy Spirit. And when we follow God and God alone, there is no telling what He can do through us as Biblical watchmen!

Matthew 15:14: "Let them alone: they be blind leaders of the blind. And if the blind lead the blind, both shall fall into the ditch."

Watchmen are not blind. We know whom we follow. We know there is not a ditch ahead, but the throne of God! We know to whom we answer. We are focused. We are actually the only ones who see things correctly in this life!

Luke 9:23-27: "And he said to *them* all, If any *man* will come after me, let him deny himself, and take up his cross daily, and follow me. For whosoever will save his life shall lose it: but whosoever will lose his life for my sake, the same shall save it. For what is a man advan-

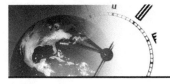

taged, if he gain the whole world, and lose himself, or be cast away? For whosoever shall be ashamed of me and of my words, of him shall the Son of man be ashamed, when he shall come in his own glory, and *in his* Father's, and of the holy angels. But I tell you of a truth, there be some standing here, which shall not taste of death, till they see the kingdom of God."

Romans 1:16: "For I am not ashamed of the gospel of Christ: for it is the power of God unto salvation to every one that believeth; to the Jew first, and also to the Greek."

Watchmen are ashamed of their pasts. They are ashamed of their sins. They are ashamed of the time they have wasted on things of this world, but they are never ashamed of the Lord Jesus Christ.

Watchmen are ashamed of their pasts. They are ashamed of their sins. They are ashamed of the time they have wasted on things of this world, but they are never ashamed of the Lord Jesus Christ. We have zeroed in on the cross. It is the center of our attention, because we know without it, we do not stand a chance to be in the presence of a holy God. So we will take up our crosses daily as we fight this battle.

Psalm 127:1: "Except the LORD build the house, they labour in vain that build it: except the LORD keep the city, the watchman waketh *but* in vain."

We know who our keeper is. It is the Lord and no one else.

Matthew 10:36-40: "And a man's foes *shall* be they of his own household. He that loveth father or mother more than me is not worthy of me: and he that loveth son or daughter more than me is not worthy of me. And he that taketh not his cross, and followeth after me, is not worthy of me. He that findeth his life shall lose it: and he that loseth his life for my sake shall find it. He that receiveth you receiveth me, and he that receiveth me receiveth him that sent me."

Once you realize that you don't belong in the world, and once the world realizes that you don't belong here as well, you have finally arrived to why you were born.

Many a watchman has been shunned by his or her family. Sadly, it can go with the territory. But a biblical watchman always knows Who receives him after his last breath!

Hebrews 11:38: "(Of whom the world was not worthy:)..."

If the world is worthy of you, you are not in the company of the watchmen of the Bible. If you fit in to this world just fine, there is a problem. Once you realize that you don't belong in the world, and once the world realizes that you don't belong here as well, you have finally arrived to why you were born. Nothing will be able to move you in the wrong direction then. The world is truly not worthy of a biblical watchman.

Revelation 12:11: "And they overcame him by the blood of the Lamb, and by the word of their testimony; and they loved not their lives unto the death."

Death just opens the door to finally see Jesus. Never forget that.

We are not merely here to take up space. We are here to make an impact everywhere we go and in everything that we do.

John 15:18-20: "If the world hate you, ye know that *it hated* me before it hated you. If ye were of the world, the world would love his own: but because ye are not of the world, but I have chosen you out of the world, therefore the world hateth you. Remember the word that I said unto you, The servant is not greater than his lord. If they have persecuted me, they will also persecute you; if they have kept my saying, they will keep yours also."

2 Timothy 3:11, 12: "Persecutions, afflictions, which came unto me at Antioch, at Iconium, at Lystra; what persecutions I endured: but out of *them* all the Lord delivered me. Yea, and all that will live godly in Christ Jesus shall suffer persecution."

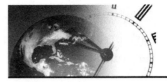

Persecution goes with the territory for a watchman. It is something our Lord had to endure as well.

Persecution goes with the territory for a watchman. It is something our Lord had to endure as well.

Proverbs 30:5: "Every word of God *is* pure: he *is* a shield unto them that put their trust in him."

Your protection is always the Lord. Keep that in the forefront of your mind.

Matthew 26:41: "Watch and pray, that ye enter not into temptation: the spirit indeed *is* willing, but the flesh is weak."

Watchmen know that they cannot let their flesh win the battle.

Luke 19:39, 40: "And some of the Pharisees from among the multitude said unto him, Master, rebuke thy disciples. And he answered and said unto them, I tell you that, if these should hold their peace, the stones would immediately cry out."

We never want the stones to be louder proclaiming eternal truth than we are. Watchmen, make sure you cry out loud and cry out strong about what the Lord has done.

1 Peter 1:7-9: "That the trial of your faith, being much more precious than of gold that perisheth, though it be tried with fire, might be found unto praise and honour and glory at the appearing of Jesus Christ: Whom having not seen, ye love; in whom, though now ye see *him* not, yet believing, ye rejoice with joy unspeakable and full of glory: Receiving the end of your faith, *even* the salvation of your souls."

A watchman can never allow the things of the world to have his affection. Be careful: The things of the world pass by very quickly.

2 Thessalonians 1:4-5: "So that we ourselves glory in you in the churches of God for your patience and faith in all your persecutions and tribulations that ye endure: *Which* is a manifest token of the righteous judgment of God, that ye may be counted worthy of the kingdom of God, for which ye also suffer:"

2 Peter 3:10-14: "But the day of the Lord will come as a thief in the night; in the which the heavens shall pass away with a great noise, and the elements shall melt with fervent heat, the earth also and the works that are therein shall be burned up. *Seeing* then *that* all these things shall be dissolved, what manner of *persons* ought ye to be in *all* holy conversation and godliness, Looking for and hasting unto the coming of the day of God, wherein the heavens being on fire shall be dissolved, and the elements shall melt with fervent heat? Nevertheless we, according to his promise, look for new heavens and a new earth, wherein dwelleth righteousness. Wherefore, beloved, seeing that ye look for such things, be diligent that ye may be found of him in peace, without spot, and blameless."

Isaiah 13:13: "Therefore I will shake the heavens, and the earth shall remove out of her place, in the wrath of the LORD of hosts, and in the day of his fierce anger."

Zephaniah 1:18: "Neither their silver nor their gold shall be able to deliver them in the day of the LORD'S wrath; but the whole land shall be devoured by the fire of his jealousy: for he shall make even a speedy riddance of all them that dwell in the land."

Revelation 12:12: "Therefore rejoice, *ye* heavens, and ye that dwell in them. Woe to the inhabiters of the earth and of the sea! for the devil is come down unto you, having great wrath, because he knoweth that he hath but a short time."

Revelation 10:6: "And sware by him that liveth for ever and ever, who created heaven, and the things that therein are, and the earth, and the things that therein are, and the sea, and the things which are therein, that there should be time no longer:"

Soon, there will be time no more. The wrath of God is about to fall in ways that have never been seen before. A watchman knows this, because a watchman knows the Word of God. The watchman must–and I do mean must–get people ready before His wrath falls.

Soon there will be time no more. The wrath of God is about to fall in ways that have never been seen before. A watchman knows this, because a watchman knows the Word of God. The watchman must–and I do mean must–get people ready before His wrath falls.

At a restaurant in Vero Beach one time, I gave the waitress a gospel tract and a $20 bill for each of the cooks and dishwashers. I wanted to bless them for their hard work and make sure they had the gospel. As I was walking out the front door, one of the cooks began to follow me. Anthony asked if I had another one of the books that I had given my waitress. He told me, "I was in the back thinking that all these people are going to die, and they don't know what awaits them, and then Liz came back and gave me the tract!" He was much more excited about the materials to reach his friends than he was the $20. He was a real watchman in the making!

> **Daniel 5:23:** "But hast lifted up thyself against the Lord of heaven; and they have brought the vessels of his house before thee, and thou, and thy lords, thy wives, and thy concubines, have drunk wine in them; and thou hast praised the gods of silver, and gold, of brass, iron, wood, and stone, which see not, nor hear, nor know: and the God in whose hand thy breath *is*, and whose *are* all thy ways, hast thou not glorified:"

When tennis legend Martina Navratilova found out she had breast cancer, she cried: "It knocked me on my [butt], really. I feel so in control of my life and my body, and then this comes, and it's completely out of my hands."[65]

God has graciously given Martina a slow death. God holds her breath in the palm of His hand. She cannot take a last breath until He says so. He gives her time to repent of her lesbianism, her pride, and her greed. The question is, will she? And the other question is, who will be the watchman in her life?

God is our protector. He is the wall of fire that will protect us as the great storms of evil come against believers in the coming days.

2 Thessalonians 1:8, 9: "In flaming fire taking vengeance on them that know not God, and that obey not the gospel of our Lord Jesus Christ: Who shall be punished with everlasting destruction from the presence of the Lord, and from the glory of his power;"

Matthew 23:37: "O Jerusalem, Jerusalem, *thou* that killest the prophets, and stonest them which are sent unto thee, how often would I have gathered thy children together, even as a hen gathereth her chickens under *her* wings, and ye would not!"

It isn't that people could not come to Jesus, but that they wouldn't. All people must be warned just like Jesus is doing here.

Zechariah 2:5: "For I, saith the LORD, will be unto her a wall of fire round about, and will be the glory in the midst of her."

God is our protector. He is the wall of fire that will protect us as the great storms of evil come against believers in the coming days. Watchmen know that they can trust the great Protector today, and that we can trust Him no matter what our eyes see in the coming days.

But please don't ever forget that watchmen are lovers. We love the Lord. We love the cross. We love the lost. Keep blowing the trumpet with all the love that you can as you warn the lost.

Live everyday like it's your last, because one day you will be right! And that is true for everyone else as well. Look at them like today could be their last day, because one day, you will be right.

It should be considered illegal for a follower of the Lord Jesus Christ not to be burning with passion for our Lord and burning with passion for the lost.

Titus 2:13: "Looking for that blessed hope, and the glorious appearing of the great God and our Saviour Jesus Christ;"

Jeremiah 20:8, 9: "For since I spake, I cried out, I cried violence and spoil; because the word of the LORD was made a reproach unto me, and a derision, daily. Then I said, I will not make mention of him, nor speak any more in his name. But *his word* was in mine heart as a burning fire shut up in my bones, and I was weary with forbearing, and I could not *stay*."

It should be considered illegal for a follower of the Lord Jesus Christ not to be burning with passion for our Lord and burning with passion for the lost. True watchmen are overflowing with this passion.

John Harper, a Baptist pastor who was on the Titanic can attest to this:

> As the rear of the huge ship began to lurch upwards, it was reported that Harper was seen making his way up the deck yelling, "Women, children and unsaved into the lifeboats!" It was only minutes later that the Titanic began to rumble deep within. Most people thought it was an explosion; actually the gargantuan ship was literally breaking in half. At this point, many people jumped off the decks and into the icy, dark waters below. John Harper was one of these people.

That night, 1,528 people went into the frigid waters. John Harper was seen swimming frantically to people in the water leading them to Jesus before the hypothermia became fatal. Mr. Harper swam up to one young man who had climbed up on a piece of debris. Rev. Harper asked him between breaths, "Are you saved?" The young man replied that he was not.

Harper then tried to lead him to Christ only to have the young man who was near shock, reply no. John Harper then took off his life jacket and threw it to the man and said, "Here then, you need this more than I do," and swam away to other people. A few minutes later, Harper swam back to the young man and succeeded in leading him to salvation. Of the 1,528 people that went into the water that night, six were rescued by the lifeboats. One of them was this young man on the debris.

Four years later, at a survivors meeting, this young man stood up and in tears recounted how that after John Harper had led him to Christ, Mr. Harper had tried to swim back to help other people, yet because of the intense cold, had grown too weak to swim. His last words before going under in the frigid waters were, "Believe on the Name of the Lord Jesus, and you will be saved.[66]

John Harper was a watchman until his very last breath. Will you be?

....

"People who don't believe in missions have not read the New Testament. Right from the beginning Jesus said the field is the world. The early church took Him at His word and went East, West, North and South."[67]
–J. HOWARD EDINGTON

"If your Gospel isn't touching others, it hasn't touched you!"[68]
—CURRY R. BLAKE

"Some wish to live within the sound of a chapel bell; I wish to run a rescue mission within a yard of hell."[69]
—C.T. STUDD

"We talk of the Second Coming; half the world has never heard of the first."[70]
—OSWALD J. SMITH

"The spirit of Christ is the spirit of missions. The nearer we get to Him, the more intensely missionary we become."[71]
—HENRY MARTYN

"We Christians are debtors to all men at all times in all places, but we are so smug to the lostness of men. We've been 'living in Laodicea,' lax, loose, lustful, and lazy. Why is there this criminal indifference to the lostness of men? Our condemnation is that we know how to live better than we are living."[72]
—LEONARD RAVENHILL

"Missionary zeal does not grow out of intellectual beliefs, nor out of theological arguments, but out of love."[73]
—ROLAND ALLEN

"Every man is a missionary, now and forever, for good or for evil, whether he intends
or designs it or not. He may be a blot radiating
his dark influence outward to the very cir-
cumference of society, or he may be a blessing, spreading benediction over the length
and breadth of the world. But a blank he cannot be: there are no moral blanks; there are
no neutral characters."[74]
–THOMAS CHALMERS

"'Not called!' did you say? 'Not heard the
call,' I think you should say. Put your ear down
to the Bible, and hear Him bid you go and
pull sinners out of the fire of sin. Put your
ear down to the burdened, agonized heart
of humanity, and listen to its pitiful wail for
help. Go stand by the gates of hell, and hear
the damned entreat you to go to their father's
house and bid their brothers and sisters and
servants and masters not to come there. Then
look Christ in the face—whose mercy you have
professed to obey—and tell Him whether you
will join heart and soul and body and circum-
stances in the march to publish His mercy to
the world."[75]
–WILLIAM BOOTH

All of the men quoted above are watchmen of the highest
regard. They had life all figured out. Will you be one of these
watchmen as well?

If you have made it this far in the book, you probably
don't hate me. But the real question is, what is your plan

of action to become the biblical watchman God has called you to be? If you are born again, you are a watchman now. Be alert, be ready, and warn everyone you can that trouble is coming if they do not repent and believe.

"'Not called!' did you say? 'Not heard the call,' I think you should say..."

–William Booth

Now it's time to put the book down. It's time to join the watch-men; time to open your mouth; time to pick up the trumpet and blow it loud and clear. Our God takes no pleasure in the death of the wicked and as one of God's watchmen neither can you. The battle has begun. ***Watchmen are needed, and they are needed now. Will you sign up to be a watchman before it is too late?***

So thou, O son of man, I have set thee a watchman unto the house of Israel; therefore thou shalt hear the word at my mouth, and warn them from me. When I say unto the wicked, O wicked man, thou shalt surely die; if thou dost not speak to warn the wicked from his way, that wicked man shall die in his iniquity; but his blood will I require at thine hand. Nevertheless, if thou warn the wicked of his way to turn from it;

if he do not turn from his way, he shall die in his iniquity; but thou hast delivered thy soul. Therefore, O thou son of man, speak unto the house of Israel; Thus ye speak, saying, If our transgressions and our sins be upon us, and we pine away in them, how should we then live? Say unto them, As I live, saith the Lord GOD, I have no pleasure in the death of the wicked; but that the wicked turn from his way and live: turn ye, turn ye from your evil ways; for why will ye die, O house of Israel?"

–Ezekiel 33:7-11

ENDNOTES

1. Oswald Chambers, <http://internationalwallofprayer.org/Q-01-FAMOUS-QUOTES.html>

2. John Wesley, <http://goodreads.com/author/quotes/151350.John_Wesley>

3. Hudson Taylor, <http://christian-quotes.ochristian.com/Hudson-Taylor-Quotes>

4. President Andrew Jackson, <http://quotationsbook.com/quote/8746>

5. Harry A. Ironside, <http://wholesomewords.org/echoes/ironsidesays.html>

6. Andy Stanley, <http://usatoday.com/news/religion/2007-10-10-christians-young_N.htm>

7. Hudson Taylor, <http://christian-quotes.ochristian.com/Hudson-Taylor-Quotes>

8. Ibid.

9. *Way of Life Encyclopedia of the Bible & Christianity*, edited by David W. Cloud, 447.

10. John Wesley, <http://thinkexist.com/quotes/john_wesley>

11. Hudson Taylor, <http://christian-quotes.ochristian.com/Hudson-Taylor-Quotes/page-3.shtml>

12. Carl Kerby, (president of Reasons for Hope, in personal correspondence)

13. Ibid.

14. Mitsuo Fuchida, <http://biblebelievers.com/fuchida1.html>

15. Dave Hunt, <http://listmyfive.com/026f0dd9/The-Top-Five-Quotes-By-Christian-Apologist-Dave-Hunt>

16. John Adams, <http://internationalwallofprayer.org/Q-01-FAMOUS-QUOTES.html>

17. John Quincy Adams, Ibid.

18. Henry Ward Beecher, Ibid.

19. George Washington Carver, Ibid.

20. Charles Colson, Ibid.

21. Joseph Cook, Ibid.

22. Cecil B. DeMille, Ibid.

23. Queen Elizabeth, Ibid.

24. Patrick Henry, Ibid.

25. Andrew Jackson, Ibid.

26. Thomas Jefferson, Ibid.

27. Helen Keller, Ibid.

28. Robert E. Lee, Ibid.

29. Abraham Lincoln, Ibid.

30. Thomas B. Macaulay, Ibid.

31. James McCosh, Ibid.

32. D.L. Moody, Ibid.

33. Dr. Robert Milikan, Ibid.

34. Malcolm Muggeridge, Ibid.

35. Napoleon, Ibid.

36. Sir Isaac Newton, Ibid.

37. Mordecai Obadiah, Ibid.

38. Bernard Ramm, Ibid.

39. Ronald Reagan, Ibid.

40. Theodore Roosevelt, Ibid.

41. Henry Thiessen, Ibid.

42. Anonymous, Ibid.

43 Anonymous, Ibid.

44 Queen Victoria, Ibid.

45 George Washington, Ibid.

46 Daniel Webster, Ibid.

47 John Wesley, Ibid.

48 Woodrow Wilson, Ibid.

49 Gene Robinson, *<http://episcopalcafe.com/lead/faith_and_politics/gene_robinsons_prayer_for_pres.html>*

50 Rick Warren, *<http://wnd.com/?pageId=86632>*

51 Barack Obama, *<http://cathleenfalsani.com/obama-on-faith-the-exclusive-interview>*

52 Pope John Paul II, *<http://transcripts.cnn.com/TRANSCRIPTS/0811/19/cnr.07.html>*

53 Billy Graham, *<http://transcripts.cnn.com/TRANSCRIPTS/0811/19/cnr.07.html>*

54 President Bush, <http://sbcbaptistpress.org/bpnews.asp?id=29507>

55 Paul Young, *The Shack*, *<http://rcmetcalf.wordpress.com/2008/11/07/hello-world>*

56 Brenda Nickel, *Basic Reformed Theology Explained And Exposed*, 73.

57 Dave Hunt, *What Love Is This?*, <http://thebereancall.org>

58 Adrian Rogers, *<http://rayfowler.org/2008/11/15/ten-great-adrian-rogers-quotes>*

59 John Wesley, Sermon #73, *<http://tentmaker.org/Quotes/hell-fire.htm>*

60 Robert Ingersoll, <http://sermonnotebook.org/new%20testament/Luke%2016_19_31.htm>

61 Peter Kirby, *<http://earlychristianwritings.com/text/martyrdompolycarp-roberts.html>*

62 Alan Carr, *<http://sermonnotebook.org/new%20testament/Luke%2016_19_31.htm>*

63 Adrian Rogers, *<http://rayfowler.org/2008/11/15/ten-great-adrian-rogers-quotes>*

64 Emily Esfahani Smith, *<http://theblaze.com/stories/this-small-mystical-stone-saved-japanese-villagers-from-tsunamis-lethal-effects>*

65 Lorenzo Benet, *<http://people.com/people/article/0,,20358261,00.html>*

66 Steve Van Nattan, *<http://blessedquietness.com/journal/housechu/harper.htm>*

67 J. Howard Edington, *<http://tentmaker.org/Quotes/evangelismquotes.htm>*

68 Curry R. Blake, Ibid.

69 C.T. Studd, Ibid.

70 Oswald J. Smith, Ibid.

71 Henry Martyn, Ibid.

72 Leonard Ravenhill, Ibid.

73 Roland Allen, Ibid.

74 Thomas Chalmers, Ibid.

75 William Booth, Ibid.

Mark Cahill has a business degree from Auburn University, where he was an honorable mention Academic All-American in basketball. He has worked in the business world at IBM and in various management positions, and he taught high school for four years. Mark now speaks to thousands of people a year at conferences, camps, retreats, etc. He has also appeared on numerous radio and television shows.

Mark's favorite thing to do is to go out and meet people and find out what they believe and why they believe it. You can find Mark at malls, concerts, art and music festivals, airports, beaches, sporting events, bar sections of towns, college campuses, etc., doing just that.

To arrange a speaking engagement,
contact the **Ambassador Agency** toll-free
at 877-425-4700 or
www.ambassadoragency.com

•

To order additional books or resources,
or to receive a free e-newsletter
www.markcahill.org

•

Contact Mark Cahill at:
P.O. Box 81, Stone Mountain, GA 30086
800-NETS-158 / 800-638-7158
Email: mark@markcahill.org